D1582059

A Systematic Approach to
GETTING RESULTS

A SYSTEMATIC APPROACH TO
GETTING RESULTS

SURYA LOVEJOY

BCA
LONDON · NEW YORK · SYDNEY · TORONTO

This edition published 1993 by BCA by arrangement with Gower Press

© Surya Lovejoy 1993

All rights reserved. The budget forms in Chapter 3 and the action management sheets shown in Chapter 6 may be photocopied for the reader's personal use only, but not for general distribution. No other part of this publication may be reproduced, stored in a retrieval system, or transmitted in any form or by any means, electronic, mechanical, photocopying, recording, or otherwise without the permission of the publisher.

CN 9013

Typeset by Ashalé Graphics and printed in Great Britain by Clays Ltd, Bungay

To everyone working on the most challenging project of them all: ending the needless death by hunger of 35 000 people a day.

CONTENTS

---

1 Turning a task into a project   1
or Know what you want to do before you try to do it

The difference between a task and a project—Defining your project—Setting the deadline—Setting the budget—Gaining agreement—Summary

---

2 Turning a project into an action plan   11
or Look before you leap

The timeline—A word about computerized project management software—Before you start—Creating a blank timeline—Filling in the timeline—The project outline—A word about risk—Contingency allowance—Completing the timeline—The critical path—Contingency planning—A word of caution—Summary

---

3 Creating and managing the budget   35
or Bean-counting for beginners

A word of reassurance—What is a budget? (1)—What is a budget? (2)—Calculating the benefits—Preparing a master budget form—A sample entry on the budget form—Filling in the budget form—Preparing a budget timeline—Adding unexpected costs—Colour coding the timeline—Recalculating the budget—Summary

---

FIGURES

PREFACE

This book has only one goal: to enhance your ability to produce results.

Getting Results is a complete handbook to the business of turning a task or goal into an accomplishment. While the tools and techniques presented in the book are taken from the field of project management, you will not be bored by academic observations or asked to try untested theories: the emphasis is entirely practical, and based firmly on proven approaches.

Chapters 1 to 7 provide a systematic approach to designing, managing and executing a project. The remaining chapters provide additional guidance on such trivia as retaining your sanity, avoiding the technology trap, coping with crisis projects and what to do when it all goes wrong.

Some of the tools may sound too simple to be of much value. Try them and see — the last thing you need when managing a complex project is a complex approach. Other tools may seem too involved. Again, try them; I promise that everything in this book is included because it works.

Finally, I would welcome your views on the *Getting Results* approach once you have had the chance to put it into practice on your own projects. You can write to me at Gower Publishing, Gower House, Croft Road, Aldershot, Hants, GU11 3HR, England.

Surya Lovejoy
London

ACKNOWLEDGEMENTS

In a book covering such a broad area as getting results, any acknowledgements are bound to be incomplete. I can only ask those not mentioned to forgive me for offering special thanks to: Caroline O'Connell, for unfailing support. Jim Ewan, for taking everything in his stride. Steve Stevenson and Jeff Reaveley, for ensuring that I face as many challenges in my leisure time as in my work. Sue Quilliam, for giving a helping hand through the publishing jungle. The Light Up Jimbolia project team, for an unforgettable Christmas. All the individuals and organizations who have contributed so freely and, sometimes, so frequently to our various charity projects. The people of The Gambia, for an inspiring example of courage, determination and vision in the face of incredible odds.

Chapter 3 owes a great deal to Simon Tovey, Finance Director of Sturge Managing Agencies; and Chapter 10 to Terry Brenig-Jones, Director of Management Arts Ltd. My thanks to them both. Any errors or omissions are, of course, my own.

A special mention is due to my wife, Caroline. Without her support and partnership, *Getting Results* would be a good idea rather than a book.

S.L.

INTRODUCTION

We are all project managers. Project management is nothing more nor less than the business of producing the results you need, when you need them – the outline job description of everyone from the caretaker to the chief executive.

Examples of typical projects include:

- organizing a conference;
- hitting a sales target;
- relocating to new premises;
- installing a new computer system;
- launching a new product;
- expanding into a new country;
- designing a new order-processing system;
- producing improved product literature;
- researching a new market;
- arranging an overseas sales trip;
- designing an in-house training course;
- evaluating future technology needs;
- drawing up contingency plans;
- recruiting new members of staff.

Literally any task can be viewed as a project (or, more accurately, *turned into* a project).

And yet, while we are offered books and training courses in everything from sales techniques to understanding management accounts, computer literacy to negotiation tools, presentation skills to power dressing, there is virtually nothing on offer covering training or guidance in the far more fundamental skill of getting results. This fact is all the more surprising given that there exists a systematic approach to the problem: project management.

The explanation for this apparent absurdity becomes obvious as soon as you pick up a standard project management text. For a field which should, above all else, be *practical*, project management instead appears to take a peculiarly academic approach to its subject. Acronyms and complex diagrams abound, making the field look like an unholy cross between a highly specialist science and an obscure form of black magic.

Getting Results is different. It takes the most effective project management tools, and presents them in a readable form that will be of genuine help to managers.

The structure of the book

Getting Results is intended to be used as a handbook, helping you to define, plan and work through a real-life project.

Chapter 1 covers a topic as vital as it is neglected: defining your project. Your project definition may well be the most important factor in determining whether you succeed or fail, so it's worth taking a little time and thought to get it right.

Chapter 2 deals with planning your project. Most of us have an understandable desire to jump straight into action with our projects, especially when time is tight. Trying to save a few days, or even hours, by failing to prepare a proper project plan, however, may well cost you weeks or months further down the line – and by then you may not have time to correct the problem. Your project plan will enable you to see exactly what has to happen when, and will identify potential problems, conflicts and emergencies *before* they arise.

Chapter 3 presents a project budgeting system designed for project managers rather than accountants. To ensure that it will be acceptable to your financial director, the system is based on conventional accountancy procedures, but it is supplemented by a unique, colour-coded budget timeline which tells you at a glance whether the project is within budget, over-budget but within your contingency allowance or over budget *and* over your planned allowances. Where the project is over budget, the budget timeline enables you to identify immediately when and how it happened.

Chapter 4 asserts that mere project *management* is not enough. A carefully dated 'to do' list may provide you with information on what needs to be done, but is unlikely to inspire you and your team to generate outstanding results – particularly once the initial novelty and excitement has worn off. Chapter 4 presents some simple yet highly effective tools for maximizing your job satisfaction during the project.

Chapter 5 tackles another neglected area: creating a winning team. While any competent manager knows how to produce results from his or her staff, most of us pay far less attention to maximizing the support of colleagues, suppliers, family and friends. Yet these people can make a significant contribution to the project given the chance. Chapter 5 details practical approaches to gaining the best possible backup from those around us.

Chapter 6 covers the nitty-gritty of turning your project plan into results. It argues that 'time management' is a myth, and provides you with a working example of an action-management system to keep your project on track and on time.

Chapter 7 gives you the weapons with which to defeat that most insidious of enemies: paperwork. Paperwork was originally intended as an aid to producing results, but is now often an enemy of, or substitute for, effective action. Chapter 7 explains how to ensure that your paperwork serves your project, and not the other way round.

Chapter 8 provides some guidance on remaining sane and avoiding burn-out during a long or fast-paced project. It is all too easy to fall into the trap of placing the project ahead of your own well-being, when the simple fact is that, without you, there *is* no project.

Chapter 9 presents some commonsense advice on making effective use of technology. Like paperwork, technology makes an excellent servant and a poor master. Chapter 9 looks at some of the main technology on offer, and presents a practical guide to the good, the bad and the ugly.

Chapter 10 deals specifically with crisis projects: projects which have to be completed without notice and to extremely tight deadlines. Crisis projects are a completely different species from projects which can be performed over a reasonable timescale, and require a totally different approach. Chapter 10 provides some appropriately brief words of advice on the art of 'quick and dirty' project management.

Chapter 11 contains guidance on what to do when things go wrong. It is short, to the point and geared to recovering from setbacks with the absolute minimum of disruption and delay.

Chapter 12 covers the steps you need to take after the project is complete. In the satisfaction and relief at achieving the objective, it is easy to forget to complete the project budget ... thank everyone involved ... even assess the value of what has been achieved. Yet these post-project actions can be every bit as important as was defining the objective at the very start. And if you are about to tackle an even bigger project, you want to be sure that you have learned every lesson possible from this one.

1

TURNING A TASK INTO A PROJECT

or Know what you want to do before you try to do it

It may sound obvious to say that you need to know what it is you want to do before you try to do it, but all of us – if we are honest – have embarked on projects, often major ones, without pausing to define our objective properly. While we may be lucky enough to get away with it, the approach is usually hit and miss, and is likely to miss at least as often as it hits.

Try a simple exercise. Think for a moment about any of the projects you will undertake during the next few months. Take a look at the resources that will be applied to the project. Make a rough guestimate of the total cost of those resources: remember to cost your own time; the time of your line managers, colleagues and your own staff; the fees of any outside consultants; all direct costs; and a percentage of overheads.

Surprising, isn't it? The chances are that even a very minor project will have a true cost running to several thousand pounds, while larger projects will run to tens or hundreds of thousands of pounds. And every penny of that money will be devoted to achieving the project goal *as you defined it at the beginning of the project*. If that definition doesn't reflect precisely what it is you are trying to do, you are risking the entire cost of the project on something which may or may not produce the results you really want.

There are, of course, some projects where it may be extremely difficult to arrive at a precise definition of the objective. A good example is adopting a new corporate image, a process which – as in the case of an organization the size of British Telecom – can cost tens of millions of pounds in direct costs, and yet may fail to produce a single penny in additional revenue.

I would suggest that *the harder it is to define the objective, the more important it is to arrive at a precise definition of that objective.* Such a process may suggest an entirely different course of action, very often one which is easier, quicker and cheaper to implement than the one planned. The corporate relaunch is again a good example. If the idea is to move into new markets, for example, would a carefully targeted advertising and direct mail campaign produce better results at a lower price?

This chapter provides you with the tools you need effectively to define your project.

The difference between a task and a project

> For a long time, it had seemed to me that life was about to begin — real life. But there was always some obstacle in the way, something to be got through first, some unfinished business, time still to be served, a debt to be paid. Then life would begin. At last it dawned on me that these obstacles *were* my life.
>
> Alfred d'Souza

Tasks are a nuisance. They get in the way of your work. At best, you clear them out of the way as quickly as possible; at worst, they accumulate to the point where you seem to spend all your time running just to stand still. Tasks also provide little guarantee of success. Since we view them as something to get out of the way, they may not be carried out properly or even at all.

A project, in contrast, is a carefully chosen objective, backed up by a well-designed plan of action. A project is designed to be satisfying, reliable and transferable. Satisfying, by providing a sense of achievement during and after its completion; reliable, by clarifying the steps and timing before you start; and transferable, by ensuring that the project definition and action plan are clear enough to enable the project to be delegated with confidence.

A project can be defined as: *A commitment to produce a specific result by a specific date and time, with the necessary actions broken down into clear, manageable steps.*

This chapter deals with the first half of this definition, the specific result by a specific date and time, while Chapter 2 deals with breaking down the necessary actions into clear, manageable steps.

Defining your project

The first step in defining your project is to canvass the views of all those involved: your customers (whose views should be paramount), senior management, colleagues and staff. Bear in mind that those close to the ground will often have valuable input, and will be much more willing to implement your plan if they were involved in its design.

Next, write down, in the simplest possible terms, what it is you are trying to achieve. Don't worry too much about the wording at this stage: it will almost certainly change several times as you work through this section.

Example objective

Despatch 95 per cent of customer orders no later than 8 a.m. the following day.

You are now going to turn your draft objective into a rock-solid project definition. You can achieve this by subjecting the draft objective to a series of eight tests. These tests are specifically designed to expose potential flaws in your objective.

Applying these tests may be uncomfortable: the objective as currently stated may be close to your heart; it may have already been communicated to others in your organization; it may have been handed down from on high. For any one of these reasons, you may be reluctant to tamper with it, preferring to gloss over any weaknesses. I can only repeat the point made at the beginning of this chapter: your project definition forms the foundation on which the entire project will be built. If there are any weaknesses, you need to know about and correct them now, not six months and £50 000 later when it may be far too late.

While it is possible to apply the tests on your own, it is far easier if you have a small group of people working on it. Three or four is the ideal number – enough of you to ensure that nothing is missed, but not so many that the exercise degenerates into chaos. Make sure that everyone understands that the objective is to end up with a bullet-proof project definition, and that they are required to be *both* merciless *and* constructive in the process of arriving at this.

Modify your objective after each test.

The customer test

How will your stated objective benefit the customer?

This question applies as much to non-commercial organizations as it does to businesses, and to internal changes as much as external ones. If the answer is that it won't, or at least only in some peripheral way, I would question the basis on which the objective was reached.

It is very easy for businesses to choose objectives like increasing turnover, profitability or market-share, rather than a customer-oriented objective – which is likely to produce these results. If you want to double your market-share, for example, you can do so only by offering potential customers a better product, an improved service or a lower price. Which of these will you do, and how will you do it?

Our sample objective above looks very customer-oriented, but is it? In talking about *despatch* rather than delivery times, the focus is on your own organization rather than the customer. This may be tempting if we use an outside courier company, and thus have no direct control over delivery times, but – from the customer viewpoint – our objective misses the point. If we really want to offer a visible improvement in your level of customer service, we need to be able to achieve a specific improvement in *delivery* times, perhaps by negotiating a customized delivery contract with our courier company.

Rewrite your objective, if necessary, from the customer viewpoint.

The means test

Does the objective specify the means by which it will be achieved?

Do you state an objective without specifying how it will be achieved? The means may be obvious to you, but this will not necessarily be true for everyone working on the project. If we are going to improve our delivery times by upgrading our order-processing system, for example, this should be stated.

Include the means in your objective.

The identity test

Does the objective make it clear who does what?

Does the objective use the words 'it', 'they', 'them' or similar? If so, replace these with the object, department, person or people concerned. This point may seem trivial, but many project managers know to their cost that different people can assume very different things when reading a simple word like 'it'.

Replace any ambiguous pronouns with actual names.

The measurement test

Is the objective measurable?

It is no good setting out to improve, increase or decrease something unless you know exactly how you will measure the improvement. What indicator will we use as our measurement, and what figure or percentage change will we achieve? If we are setting out to deliver 95 per cent of orders to our customers' premises by 12 noon on the day after the order was received, for example, how will we know whether or not we are achieving this?

The measurement should be defined as tightly as possible. In our delivery example, we could not rely on customer complaints, for example: many customers would not complain, but merely put up with it for a while before switching to a new supplier.

In some cases we may already collect the measurements we need; in other cases, we may have to design a measuring system – for example, phoning a random sample of customers to check the time of delivery.

Anything can be measured, even 'soft' factors like customer satisfaction. You could, for example, simply ask your customers to rate your service on a scale from 0 to 100. While you would want to back this up with questions about specific aspects of your service, the overall rating is one of the best possible guides to overall satisfaction because it is based on *customer* perceptions – and that is what counts. A suitable customer-service objective might be to increase your average satisfaction rating from X per cent to Y per cent, with *nobody* rating their satisfaction lower than Y – 20 per cent.

Working without measurements is like flying an aeroplane without flight instruments: it *can* be done, but not reliably and safely, and not if you intend to live long enough to collect your pension.

Modify your objective, if necessary, to include (a) the method of measurement and (b) the figure or percentage improvement to be achieved.

The sufficiency test

Are there any circumstances in which achieving the objective would not be enough?

Imagine that you have achieved your objective – as it is currently defined. Now think about possible circumstances in which that achievement could be insufficient, or even irrelevant. For example, it may be relatively easy to achieve faster order-processing and despatch at the expense of accuracy but your customers may not consider it an improvement, however, to receive the wrong goods an hour early.

Include in your objective any additional relevant factors.

The side-effect test

Could achieving the objective produce any adverse side-effects?

As before, imagine that you have achieved your objective as it is currently defined. Think about how it will have been achieved. Now think about what side-effects may result. An obvious one is a hidden or unforeseen increase in costs. Less obvious, but potentially far more serious, is a decline in working conditions for staff. If our new order-processing system results in staff dissatisfaction, for example, then at best you are likely to find your customers receiving a less friendly service, and at worst you may risk industrial action or even the resignation of key staff.

This test underlines the importance of careful thought at the project definition stage: eliminating an undesirable side-effect at this point can be as simple as adding a sentence to the brief given to a systems analyst; trying to remove the same side-effect once the system is up and running may take months and cost tens of thousands of pounds.

Modify or add to the objective to take account of the side-effects you identified.

The assumption test

Are you basing your objective on untested assumptions?

Are you assuming that a particular change will result in a particular effect? For example, are you assuming that faster delivery times will result in increased orders? If so, what evidence do you have for your assumption? Suitable evidence would include past experience, the experience of competitors (so long as you can be sure that your data is accurate) and customer surveys. If you do *not* have any suitable evidence, it may be worthwhile testing the assumption – even if it seems obvious – before embarking on a long and costly project. Remember that generalizations are only *generally* true.

If your objective makes untested assumptions, test them before proceeding.

The jargon test

Can the objective be understood by everyone involved?

It is vital that everyone working on the project, no matter how minor a role they may have, understands what it is you are trying to achieve. The objective should be written in plain English, taking care to avoid jargon and assumed knowledge.

Test the wording on your most junior member of staff, and reword if required.

If your objective now passes all eight of the above tests, you have the first half of your project definition: a commitment to produce a specific result.

Setting the deadline

An objective without a deadline is likely to be achieved slowly or not at all. When things are busy, which in today's business world is all of the time, anything without a deadline tends to go straight to the bottom of the pile. For this reason, if a project does not have a deadline, it is essential to create one.

Whether the deadline is decided for you or you set it yourself, you need to be sure that it is realistic: that the necessary actions can be completed in the time available, given the resources available. If not, you need to know this at the earliest possible stage in order to decide what you will do about it: move the deadline, redefine the project or obtain additional resources.

Conversely, you need to be equally sure that it does not allow *too much* time. While a certain amount of leeway is vital (only Swiss trains run precisely to schedule), it is equally important to maintain the momentum of a project through a reasonably tight deadline. Even if there is no objective reason for the deadline, make sure that you take it seriously so that others do. A deadline need reflect nothing more than an urgent commitment to create or correct something.

Do not worry if your deadline seems arbitrary – just as you refined your draft objective in this chapter, so you will refine your deadline in the next. The important thing at this stage is to make sure that you have a deadline, even one picked out of the air.

Setting the budget

Budgets are almost always determined for us, either from above or simply by the organization's cash-flow. As with the deadline, however, you want to be sure that the budget is realistic. And again, too much money is as much a danger as too little: surplus money not only encourages waste, but also reduces the satisfaction of completing the project – after all, anyone can achieve anything if they can throw enough money at it. (This, incidentally, is one of the reasons corporate managers are so often attracted to the idea of running their own business: it may be tough learning to produce professional results on a budget a fraction of the size of your larger competitors, but there is a tremendous satisfaction in pulling it off.)

If you are already experienced in financial management, use your own systems for budgeting. Otherwise, use the system described in Chapter 3.

Gaining agreement

There is little point in taking great pains over the project definition if there is a danger of it being arbitrarily changed once the project is in motion. It is thus essential to gain the approval and agreement of all those involved in the decision right at the outset.

You have already invited the *views* of everyone concerned; now you need to gain their agreement and co-operation.

Most important of all is to gain the full agreement of anyone with the power to interfere with the project once you have started work on it: your immediate boss, and all those above him or her. This requires a diplomatic approach: your line manager would probably not take too kindly to your going over his head to talk to the chairman – go through your manager, politely but carefully asking whether everyone with a potential interest in the project has approved the definition.

SUMMARY

- Tasks are unreliable and a nuisance; projects are satisfying, reliable and transferable.

- A project is a commitment to produce a specific result by a specific date and time, with the necessary actions broken down into clear, manageable steps.

- The entire resources assigned to a project are assigned to the job of achieving the objective as you defined it at the beginning of the project. If the project definition fails to hit the mark, those resources are being risked on a gamble.

- The more difficult it is to arrive at a specific definition, the more important it is to do so.

- The first step in defining a project is to canvass the views of all those involved, including two neglected groups: customers, and staff close to the ground.

- Write down, in the simplest possible terms, exactly what it is you are trying to achieve, then work through the tests given in this chapter.

- Set a deadline which is realistic, yet tight enough to demand urgent action.

- Set a budget which is realistic, yet tight enough to avoid waste and ensure a sense of satisfaction.

- Get the agreement and approval of everyone with the power to interfere with the project once it is up and running.

2

TURNING A PROJECT INTO AN ACTION PLAN

or Look before you leap

In the book *The Hitchhiker's Guide to the Galaxy*, there is a device known as the 'infinite improbability drive'. It works on the principle that, since anything – no matter how unlikely – has a finite probability, absolutely *everything* will eventually happen of its own accord given the right combination of circumstances. All you need do, therefore, is calculate the odds against your desired objective happening all on its own, and feed this figure into the device.

Sadly, the infinite improbability drive is not yet commercially available. Today's project managers must therefore use the less exciting but perhaps more reliable method of creating an action plan, or timeline.

The timeline

> Keep in mind always the present you are constructing. It should be the future you want.
>
> Alice Walker

A timeline is a visual summary of what needs to happen when. It can take many forms. At its simplest, it can be little more than a simple, dated 'to do' list. At its most sophisticated, it can be a computerized critical-path analysis. It can take the form of a list, a table or a computer-style flowchart. It might list fewer than ten actions, or tens of thousands. It may span a few days, or more than ten years. It might be small enough to fit inside a personal organizer, or it may cover an entire office wall (the timeline for the Concorde project took up the entire length of an aircraft hangar wall!).

Whatever its form, the purpose of a timeline is to provide an at-a-glance overview of the project. It should make clear sequences, priorities and responsibilities.

Sequences

The order in which things happen is often vital. If you are organizing a conference, for example, you cannot book the catering until you know the venue; you cannot book the venue until the dates have been finalized; and you cannot confirm the dates until you have checked the availability of your key speakers.

Priorities

Some actions are more important than others. A delay in, or even the omission of, one action may have little or no effect on the progress of the project as a whole, while even the briefest of delays in a *key* action may stop the entire project in its tracks. In the conference example, a delay in preparing some overhead projection slides will not become critical until a few days before the conference, while a delay in choosing your keynote speaker will delay virtually all other actions. It is therefore essential to prioritize those actions which have the greatest impact on the progress of the project as a whole.

Responsibilities

The surest route to disaster is to allow confusion or doubt over who will do what. We have all experienced occasions when something did not happen because everyone thought somebody else was doing it; that 'something' just might turn out to be confirming the keynote speaker . . .

The timelining system presented in this chapter satisfies all these requirements. It has a proven track record, and has the additional virtues of being simple to use and inexpensive to create.

A word about computerized project management software

You will find a discussion of the pros and cons of project planning software in Chapter 9. All I want to say here is: beware! While such systems are superficially attractive, and can be extremely useful at the project *planning* stage, they are not, in my view, suitable for the project *management* process. I strongly recommend reading Chapter 9 before committing yourself to such a system.

Before you start

You'll need a few tools before you can begin creating the timeline described below. All are readily available:

- lightweight card: some 63 x 51cm sheets (this is a common size). The amount you will need depends on the length and complexity of your project, but as a rough guide allow one sheet for each week of the project for projects lasting up to two months, and one sheet for each month of the project for projects lasting over two months. For projects involving more than six people or departments, double the amount. In all cases, get enough spare sheets to allow for mistakes, and more paper than you expect to use: it is inexpensive and anything left over will be useful next time. You will also need plenty of A4 paper (copier paper is ideal);
- blue-tac or similar: some method of fixing the paper to your office wall. You should, of course, check that the product you choose is suitable for the surface of your wall;
- coloured marker pens: felt markers, OHP pens, etc. You will need two sets, each containing at least four, and preferably eight, different colours. One set should be fine tipped, around 0.5 mm, and the other medium to thick, around 10 mm. You will also need a highlighter pen;
- removable sticky notes: post-it notes or similar, in the smallest size (5 cm x 4 cm). You will use one note per action, so make sure you have plenty of pads. Stick to a single colour; white looks neatest;
- a long ruler.

Buy plenty of everything – nothing is more frustrating than having to interrupt your planning because you have run out of paper or a pen has dried up!

Creating a blank timeline

All but the simplest of projects will involve several simultaneous tracks: different categories of action each with its own person or team in charge. In our conference example, the categories or tracks might be: Speakers and VIPs, Participants, Logistics, Admin, and

Other. In a new product development, the categories might be Market Research, Product Research, Consumer Testing, Finance, Marketing and Sales. These categories or tracks are usually decided for you by the structure of the organization.

You would typically have a maximum of nine or ten tracks, including one called **Project Management** and another called **Other** (the reason for these tracks will become apparent a little later). You can, however, have more than ten tracks if you like.

The first stage in creating your blank timeline is to divide the project into its different tracks. Each track will be represented by a row on your timeline grid. Take a sheet of card, and draw the grid shown in Figure 2.1.

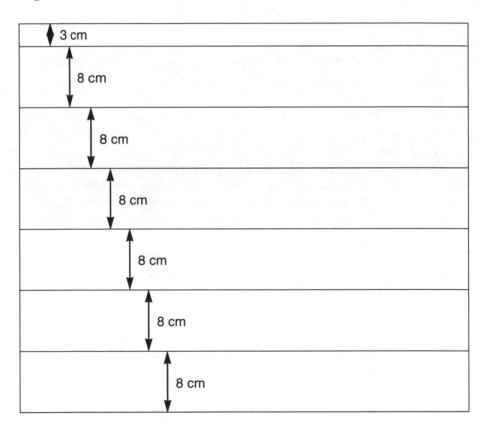

Figure 2.1 Project planning grid: title sheet

Next, write in the name of each track, together with the name of the person or department accountable for that track. The top track should be labelled 'Project Management' and the bottom one 'Other'. Use a different coloured pen for each track (Figure 2.2).

Project Management	Adrian Wood
Speakers & VIPs	Susan Dennis
Participants	Carole Bunting
Logistics	Richard Ellis
Admin	Chris Walker
Other	

Figure 2.2 Labelling the project planning grid

The colour coding is important as you will use it throughout the project, for everything from sling files to progress-report covers. If you do not have enough colours, use stripes or other patterns to create a unique colour coding for each track. If this colour coding seems like an unnecessary complication or luxury, its value will become increasingly apparent as the volume of paperwork grows!

The next decision to make is the units of time you will use. For a project lasting up to two months, I recommend a timescale divided into days. For longer projects, I suggest weeks. Your units of time will be represented by columns down the timeline grid.

Take a fresh sheet. Draw the track lines across the sheet exactly as before (see Figure 2.1). Now divide the sheet into columns.

Working in days

You should have seven columns: Monday to Sunday (even if you normally work a five-day week, there may be some work that needs to be done over a weekend – particularly towards the end of the project). Mark the day of each column at the top of the Project Management track, but do not add any dates – these will come later (see Figure 2.3). You will need one of these sheets for each week of the project. Number each sheet for ease of reference.

SHEET 01

MON	TUE	WED	THU	FRI	SAT	SUN
◄— 9 cm —►						

Figure 2.3 Project planning grid: daily version

Working in weeks

I recommend having four weeks per sheet. You will later mark the Week Beginning date at the top of the Project Management track, but leave this blank for the moment (Figure 2.4). You will need one of these sheets for each four weeks of the project. Number each sheet for ease of reference. When working in weeks, produce an additional sheet divided into days (see Figure 2.3) to represent the current week.

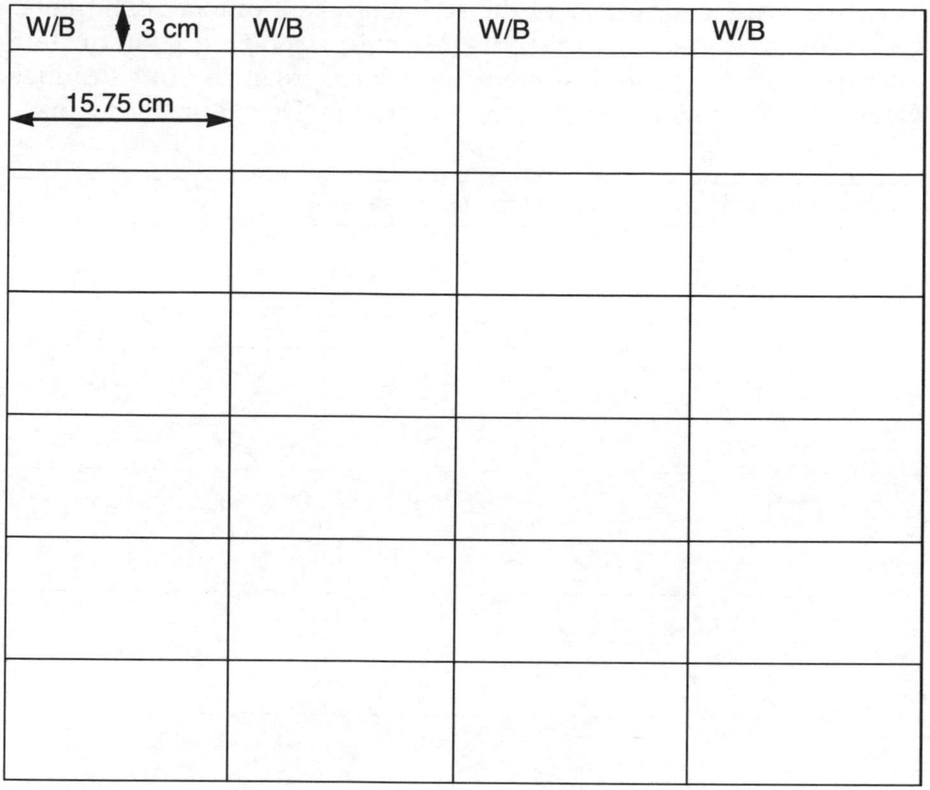

W/B ↕ 3 cm	W/B	W/B	W/B
←—— 15.75 cm ——→			

Figure 2.4 Project planning grid: weekly version

If you have more than six project tracks, create additional sheets as appropriate (Figure 2.5).

You now have your blank timeline, and are ready to begin planning the project.

Filling in the timeline

Actions and events are placed on to the timeline using Post-It notes (or similar). This is both easier than writing directly on to the timeline itself, especially once it is on your office wall, and also makes it easy to move items if you have to reschedule later: you can just lift off the Post-It note and reposition it on the new date. You can do the same thing if you transfer responsibility for an action, for example if you decide that the marketing team should handle a direct mail operation rather than the sales team.

You will write a summary of the action or event onto a Post-It note. Use coloured pens to match your colour coding system. For example, if you have assigned the colour green to your Product Development track, use green ink for Product Development actions.

(this area will be overlapped by the sheet above)			

Figure 2.5 Project planning grid: additional tracks

Actions which *must* be completed on or by a certain date will be underlined.

There are two stages to filling in the timeline: first, creating the project outline (a summary of the results you will need to achieve along the way); second, inserting the action steps themselves.

The project outline

The project outline is a list of the main results you will need to produce in order to complete the project. In a product development project, for example, the project outline might look like this:

- consumer research complete;
- product specifications agreed;
- draft design complete;
- prototype produced;
- alpha tests complete;
- beta test sites arranged;
- beta tests complete;
- beta site feedback analysed;
- production specification complete.

You can see that, while this list contains no information on how these results will be achieved, it does illustrate the approach you will take and give you a good idea of what needs to be achieved. In conventional project management, these intermediate results are generally known as *milestones*.

The way in which you will create your project outline will vary depending on the size and complexity of the project. If you are responsible for the project on your own, you will choose the outline yourself. If you have a small team, you will create it in a team meeting. If you have a large team, with a number of departments or organizations involved, you will ask the head of each department or organization to produce a draft outline for each track, and then bring everything together in a meeting of the team leaders.

Choosing your milestones

Whichever approach you take, the guidelines for choosing your milestones are the same.

1. There is no magic formula for identifying your milestones: *you* choose them. They should represent achievements or stages that make sense to you and your team.

2. Milestones should be frequent. They will act both as checkpoints and as 'celebration' points along the way. To a large extent, they will determine the sense of satisfaction you get from the project: infrequent milestones will make it seem as if progress is slow, while frequent ones will generate a sense of urgency and velocity.

This is particularly important with longer projects: a sense of momentum and satisfaction during the project is vital to morale – not only that of the team, but also your own.

3. You should always have a milestone at the point where different tracks meet. For example, 'Brochure Complete' might mark a point where Design, Marketing and Technical Writing tracks meet.

Start with scrap paper and begin listing possible milestones. Use the 'brainstorm' technique: write down everything you think of, without judgement or discussion, in any old order. This technique is particularly effective with a group of people, but make sure everyone understands that the point is simply to create a list of possibilities, not to pass judgement on any of them (Figure 2.6).

```
Speakers:                         Participants:

Target list drawn up              Mailing list sources
All speakers contacted            identified
All responses received            All mailing lists in house
                                  Mailshot material ready

                                  (etc.)
```

Figure 2.6 'Brainstorming' possible milestones

Once you have run out of ideas, take a fresh sheet of paper and transfer the ones you want to use. You might want to take a little time to discuss the pros and cons, but do not get too caught up in long-winded discussion – and let the team leader of each track have the final say on that track's milestones.

Once you have your chosen milestones, use a rough timeline grid to place them into sequential order, and to separate them by track. Do not worry at all about the dates of the actions – you will work out these in a moment – just get everything into the right order and the right track.

Check for relationships between the tracks: there will almost certainly be occasions on which one track cannot begin or continue its work on a milestone until another track has completed one of its milestones. In the product development example, above, the Product Design team cannot agree the specifications until the Market Research team has completed its analysis of the consumer research. These factors will affect the sequence of the project as a whole.

There may be some milestones where it is not clear to which track it belongs. If so, look first to see if one of the existing teams/team members should handle it by virtue of their expertise or experience. Make sure, however, that you do not over-burden a particular team or individual with additional work. If the milestone cannot be assigned to one of the existing tracks, place it in the Other track and make a note that you will have to find somebody to manage it (Figure 2.7).

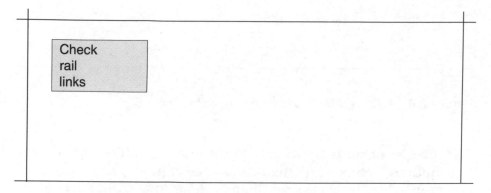

Figure 2.7 Project milestones

You now have your project outline and are ready to begin the final stage of creating your timeline: inserting the action steps themselves.

Inserting the action steps

As with the milestones, the approach you will take to inserting the action steps depends on the size and complexity of the project: you might complete this stage on your own, in a team meeting or by asking each team to prepare the actions for its own track.

Whichever approach you take, the process is the same. Take a piece of A4 paper for each milestone, and write the milestone at the top.

Then, for each milestone, write down the individual actions required to achieve the result. These should be in sequential order (Figure 2.8).

BROCHURE TO PRINTER

Decide on format of brochure.

Get quotes from printer.

Choose and book printer.

Design brochure (Melanie).

Write draft text (Bill).

Send text for approval (Dave, Sarah, John).

Write final text.

Send job to printer.

Figure 2.8 Actions required to achieve a milestone

The level of detail is up to you, but it must be sufficient to ensure that nothing can be forgotten. As a general guide, any individual action which will take longer than an hour to complete should be included.

If you find that a milestone has more than ten actions, or spans more than a week, I recommend breaking it down into several different milestones. For example, Consumer Research Complete might break down into Consumer Questionnaire Complete, Research Completed and Research Analysis Complete.

You now need to know how long each action will take. There are four main ways you can estimate this:

- your own experience;
- the experience of the individuals/teams responsible;
- similar projects completed in the past;
- specialist advice.

Wherever possible, use more than one source for each estimate: for example, your own experience, the estimate of the team responsible and the evidence of past projects.

If you know your team, you will know how reliable each person's estimates are likely to be; you may know that Fred always delivers a week late, Jane covers herself with over-cautious estimates and usually delivers in half the time and John will always deliver the goods on time but needs to be chased on a daily basis. Take these factors into account. If you do not know the team, try to get some informal guidance from a previous manager, remembering that this will be less reliable than direct personal experience.

The same thing applies to work performed by outside contractors. Although you may, in principle, be covered by contracts and penalty clauses, recovering some or all of your money if a contractor fails to deliver will be of little comfort at the time. Again, time estimates as well as cost estimates should be sought from more than one supplier, and again use your own and other people's experience of similar projects. Write the estimated time alongside each action step.

A word about risk

The safest course in drawing up your timeline is to use the most pessimistic estimate for each action. In practice, however, this may not be feasible: you will often be under pressure to meet a tight deadline, and the most pessimistic times could suggest that a three-month project is going to take the best part of three years!

The bad news, therefore, is that committing to your timeline will inevitably involve risk. Even using the most pessimistic times does not eliminate this risk – the unexpected could still occur. The good news is that, while you cannot avoid risk, you can control it.

The golden rule in committing to a timeline is to *ensure that the degree of risk reflects the potential consequences*. If the consequences of failing to meet a particular deadline would be catastrophic, you should ensure that the risk is small. In other words, use the most pessimistic estimate. If the consequences of failing to meet another deadline would be inconsequential, you can afford to risk a less pessimistic deadline. You should still, however, aim for realism rather than optimism.

Check your estimated times to ensure that you are following the golden rule.

Contingency allowance

Nothing ever goes according to plan. While your time estimates should be realistic, and erring on the safe side, they still cannot be relied upon. You should therefore add a contingency allowance to the estimated time for each action.

Experienced project managers on familiar territory generally include a 10 per cent contingency allowance; those less experienced should allow 20 per cent.

You will also need to make specific contingency plans so that you will know what to do when something goes wrong – we will come to this at the end of the chapter.

Completing the timeline

Now that you have your complete action list, together with a time estimate for each action, you can complete your timeline. You do this by transferring the milestones from the rough timeline to the final one, and by inserting the action steps between each of the milestones. This will provide you with a complete, detailed plan of the project, with every action under the appropriate date.

Timelines are normally completed *backwards*. In other words, you start with the end result and work in reverse order towards the start. This approach assumes that the deadline is fixed, and calculates the point at which you need to begin work on the project.

Take one of your blank timeline sheets, and date it for the week or month of the deadline as in Figure 2.9.

Transfer the last milestone of the project from the rough timeline to the final one. Use a highlighter pen to identify the item as a milestone. Place it in the day or week of the project deadline. (If you have any doubts about your time estimates, and think that your contingency allowance still may be insufficient, you can allow extra leeway at this stage by placing the final milestone some time *before* the actual deadline. Do not overdo it, however: if you have followed the advice given earlier, you should be fine.)

Now work *backwards* through the actions for this milestone. Take each action and write it on to a Post-It note. Use coloured pens to identify the track: this makes it easier to make sense of the timeline at a glance.

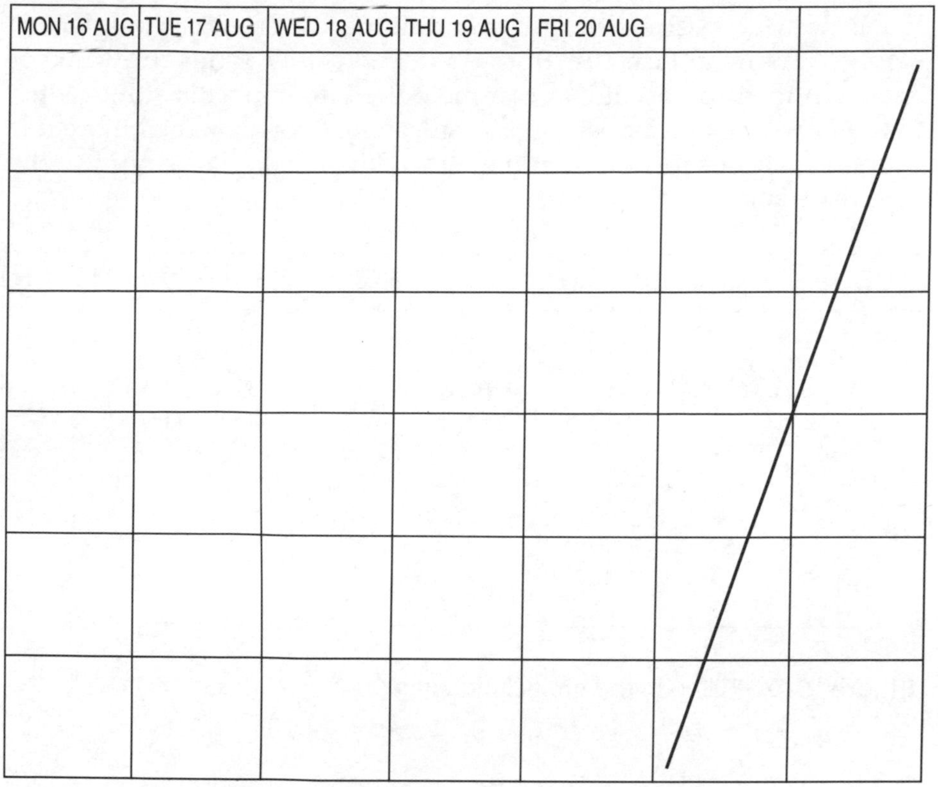

MON 16 AUG	TUE 17 AUG	WED 18 AUG	THU 19 AUG	FRI 20 AUG			

Figure 2.9 Project planning grid for the end of the project

At the bottom of the note, write in the time required for the action, expressed in days or fractions of an eight-hour working day. Thus two hours becomes 0.25 of a working day. While this may seem slightly fiddly at this stage, you will appreciate it later!

Finally, position the action on the timeline. Simply note the time required for the action, and count backwards from the milestone. For example, if the milestone is Thursday, 10 June 1993, and the final action takes two working days, count back two days and place the action on Tuesday, 8 June (Figure 2.10). Use additional Post-It notes to connect the actions and milestones with arrows, as shown in Figure 2.10. Remember to count only working days: if the action had required four days, you would count back four working days to Friday, 4 June.

Now repeat the process for each action belonging to this milestone. Once this is complete, put the paper to one side (do not throw it away – file it in case anything happens to the timeline) and move on to the next milestone in this track.

If a milestone requires input from another track, for example, the Design Team needs the Beta-Test Feedback from the Market Research team before it can complete the Final Specification, switch to the new track and position the milestone about a week before it is needed (another form of contingency allowance). Then return to the original track.

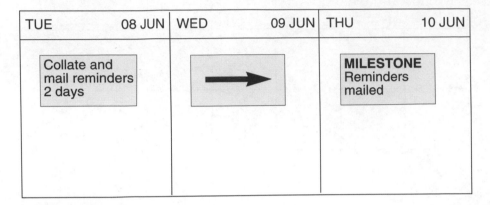

Figure 2.10   Filling in the project planning grid

Add new (earlier) project planning grids as required. Date each one as you use it. You may find it useful to stick them together with sticky tape on the back.

When you have completed the first track, move on to the next.

If there is a lot of interaction between the different tracks, you may have to do some adjusting as you go. You may, for example, find that a particular milestone has to be achieved a week earlier in order to meet the needs of another track. This is where the Post-It notes come into their own – it is a simple matter to peel them off and move them back a week.

The critical path

We said at the beginning of the chapter that a timeline has to satisfy three criteria: it has to show sequence, priorities and responsibilities. Our timeline as it stands satisfies two of these: it shows sequence and responsibilities. It does not, however, yet show priorities. We will now correct this in order to complete the timeline.

There are a number of situations in life where somebody somewhere has taken a perfectly simple concept and given it a horrendously complex-sounding name. Critical-path analysis is one of these. Do not be deterred; critical-path analysis is just a fancy term for identifying the most urgent tasks. And now that you have your timeline complete working out the critical path is a simple process.

First, identify the milestones where all the tracks meet (that is, they all have the same milestone). This may happen only at the end of the project, or it may happen frequently throughout the project; it does not matter which.

Second, for each track, add up the total number of days required between each of these milestones, as shown for example in Figure 2.11.

W/B 08 FEB	W/B 15 FEB	W/B 22 FEB	W/B 01 MAR
			Phase one complete
uuuuuuuuuu uuuuuuu 2 days	uuuuuuuuuu uuu 2 days	uuuuuuuuuu uuuuuuuuuu 4 days	All speakers finalized (8 days)
uuuuuuuuuu uuuuuuuuuu 5 days	uuuuuuuuuu uuuuu 1 day	uuuuuuuuuu 0.5 days	Numbers finalized (6.5 days)
uuuuuuuuuu uuu 4 days	uuuuuuuuuu uuuuuuu 4 days	uuuuuuuuuu uuu 3 days	Venue details finalized (11 days)
uuuuuuuuuu uuuuuuuu 5 days	uuuuuuuuuu uuuuuuuuu 4 days	uuuuuuuuuu uuuuu 4 days	Admin systems ready (13 days)

Figure 2.11 Identifying the critical path

The track with the highest number of days is the 'critical path' (most urgent track) for that section of the project. You should identify the critical path by running a highlighter pen across the top of each

Post-It note on the relevant track. Remember, if there are several points where the tracks meet, you have only worked out the critical path for one section of the project, and should only highlight the actions in that section (Figure 2.12).

W/B 08 FEB	W/B 15 FEB	W/B 22 FEB	W/B 01 MAR
			Phase one complete
uuuuuuuuuu *uuuuuuu* 2 days	*uuuuuuuuuu* *uu* 2 days	*uuuuuuuuuu* *uuuuuuuu* 4 days	All speakers finalized (8 days)
uuuuuuuuuu *uuuuuuuuu* 5 days	*uuuuuuuuuu* *uuuu* 1 day	*uuuuuuuuuu* 0.5 days	Numbers finalized (6.5 days)
uuuuuuuuuu *uuu* 4 days	*uuuuuuuuuu* *uuuuuuu* 4 days	*uuuuuuuuu* *uu* 3 days	Venue details finalized (11 days)
▬▬▬▬▬▬ *uuuuuuuuu* 5 days	▬▬▬▬▬▬ *uuuuuuuuu* 4 days	▬▬▬▬▬▬ *uuuuu* 4 days	Admin systems ready (13 days)

Figure 2.12 Highlighting the critical path

Now, what happens next is certainly easier to do than it is to explain, so take it slowly. The critical path shows you which track needs the longest time for any given section of the project. It is called the critical path because any delay in this track will delay the rest of the project.

Since all the other tracks require *less* time for that section, they have some leeway – what the Americans call 'slack time'. The difference between the time required for the critical track, and the time required for A N Other track is the 'slack time' of the A N Other track.

In the example shown by Figure 2.11, the admin track is the critical path. It requires 13 days. The Speakers track, in contrast, requires only 8 days. The difference between the two is five days, so the Speakers track is said to have five days' slack time for that section of the project. In other words, the Speakers team could take up to five days longer to complete that section without delaying the rest of the project.

Work out the slack time for each track, and mark this on an additional Post-It note for each track as in Figure 2.13.

Repeat the process for each section of the timeline in which all the tracks meet. The highlighted actions now illustrate the critical path of your project. It may run in a single track from start to finish, or it may run through a

W/B	01 MAR
Phase one complete	
All speakers finalized (8 days)	Slack time: (5 days)
Numbers finalized (6.5 days)	Slack time: (6.5 days)
Venue details finalized (11 days)	Slack time: (2 days)
Admin systems ready (13 days)	Critical path

Figure 2.13 Calculating the 'slack time' for each path

different track at different stages of the project. In either case, it serves two purposes.

1. Whenever there is a conflict between two or more tracks – perhaps different teams require use of the same computer system at the same time, for example – the critical path will instantly reveal which track should be given priority.

2. Whenever a track is delayed, you will be able to see at a glance how this will effect the overall running of the project. If the delay is in the critical path, you know that it is urgent and must be minimized as a matter of priority. If it is *not* in the critical path, the slack time will tell you whether or not the delay poses a risk to the project: a delay lower than the slack time poses no risk, while a delay greater than the slack time poses the same risk as a delay in the critical path and should be prioritized accordingly.

Contingency planning

You have already included a contingency allowance – extra time to allow for things to go wrong – but this only gives you enough time to solve the problem, it does not tell you *how* to solve it. And the middle of an emergency is not the best time in the world to think through a problem with a cool head!

Contingency plans are alternative action plans that will come into effect if the intended plan goes wrong. You develop these plans ahead of time so that there is no panic or delay during the emergency itself: you simply move straight into the contingency plan. With careful preparation, rehearsal and execution, it is possible to execute a contingency plan for a major disaster without anyone beyond your team even noticing the disaster.

As with most things in the field of project management, developing contingency plans is a straightforward process, but needs to be done carefully. It is simply a matter of running through your action plan and examining each action in turn. Ask yourself (and others) what could go wrong with the action. For example, if an action states that your printer will deliver 50000 copies of a product brochure on 15 March, there are various opportunities for Murphy's Law to enter the fray. The printer might deliver late – anything from a few hours to a few weeks. They might deliver only 20000 copies. They might have made a serious error which requires a complete reprint (although this should have been averted by proper proofing procedures). They might even have burnt down or gone bust before beginning the job!

Once you know what might go wrong, you can develop a contingency plan for each possibility: an alternative plan of action that would solve the problem. It would, of course, be impractical to cover every single eventuality: you would never get a chance to begin work on the project! Only a handful of key actions require 'bomb-proof' (sometimes literally!) contingency plans which are every bit as detailed and carefully thought through as the intended plan. At the other end of the scale, a contingency plan might be nothing more than a quick phone call to check that another supplier could step in at short notice if required. Or even, in the case of trivial actions, a decision to accept the failure without correcting it.

The amount of time and resources you should devote to developing and preparing a contingency plan depends on two factors:

1. the degree of risk involved (that is, how likely is it that something will go wrong with the original plan?);

2. the consequences of a failure in the original plan (that is, how much damage would the failure do to the project as a whole?).

Clearly if the risk is high and the consequences are serious, you should have a complete, detailed contingency plan ready to roll. You may also want a detailed contingency plan if the risk is small but the consequences disasterous: it may be unlikely that the keynote speaker will fail to arrive, particularly given that you will have arranged for him to arrive the previous afternoon and be put up at a nearby hotel overnight, but you would certainly want to have an alternative speaker ready to step into the breach just in case. At the other extreme, if the risk is virtually non-existent and the consequences trivial, it is not worth wasting resources on a detailed contingency plan.

You can assess both risk and consequences in the same way as you assigned completion times to each action in your timeline: use your own and other peoples' experience of similar projects, as well as any specialist advice available. In the absence of any of the above, commonsense is generally a good guide, but not always . . .

The computer company Digital Equipment agreed to supply and run a computerized results system for the London Marathon. Since the computer systems were sited in a caravan on Westminster Bridge, it was decided to provide power from a dedicated generator craned in for the occasion, the Digital engineers considering it too risky to rely on the mains power supply. Since uninterrupted power was critical to the success of the project, the project team went so far as to install a back-up generator also. Most people considered this a needless extravagance: the size of generator required to operate the computers was expensive, and the chances of a power cut right in the very heart of London during the few hours of the marathon were, they said, inconceivably small. Digital went ahead anyway, and the team had the smuggest expressions for miles around when the inconceivable happened, the Westminster area suffered a power failure just as the Marathon was getting under way, and the computers hummed away happily as if nothing had happened.

For extremely critical actions, you may even have more than one contingency plan. It is not unusual to prepare a detailed contingency plan which you expect to use if something goes wrong, and then back this up with a further 'last resort' alternative in case the contingency plan fails also! Typically, the 'last resort' plan will be extremely crude: if things have gone *that* badly wrong, you want something so simple it cannot possibly fail. Again, Digital did this during the Marathon. Its standard contingency against computer failure was a second computer system set up as a 'hot backup' (that is one that is receiving the same data as the first, and can instantly take over when required with no loss of data or performance). Digital backed this up with a 'last resort' contingency of a primarily manual system comprising a standalone wordprocessor and a hardcopy printout of the complete runner database. This system was capable of providing the essential results required on the day itself. Each person on the team had been assigned an alternative role involving extensive manual processing. Thanks to the uninterruptible power supply, this last-ditch alternative was not required, but it did provide the team with considerable peace of mind.

Bear in mind that some contingency plans need to be worked into the main action plan. In the case of the London Marathon, Digital had to design the 'hot backup' into the system right from the start, and they had to train everyone in, and rehearse, the manual system in case it was needed. You may, therefore, need to update your action plan accordingly.

Finally, when your contingency plans are complete, you should ensure that everyone on the team knows what event will trigger each contingency plan (at what point will you consider that the original plan is no longer viable?) and what role they will play in implementing it.

A word of caution

Detailed planning can be fiddly and boring. It can be tempting to rush the process, particularly when time is tight. Please don't! The timeline is the difference between a project that is under control and one which is out of control. The time you invest now in careful planning will repay you tenfold once the project is under way, and may ultimately mean the difference between success and failure.

If time is short, getting your planning right is *more* rather than less important: when you have plenty of time, you can afford to waste time by getting it wrong; when time is short, you have to get it right first time. It is worth it, I promise.

SUMMARY

- A timeline is a visual summary of what needs to happen when. It should make clear sequences, priorities and responsibilities.

- All but the simplest project will involve several simultaneous 'tracks'. These tracks are represented by horizontal rows on the timeline. Tracks are colour coded for ease of reference.

- Timelines can have different units of time, depending on the length of the project. For projects lasting up to two months, use a timeline divided into days; for longer projects, use weeks instead. Units of time are represented by vertical columns on the timeline.

- A project outline is a list of the main results you will need to achieve in order to complete the project. These intermediate results are known as milestones.

- There is no magic formula for determining the project milestones – choose ones that make sense to you. They should, however, be frequent since they act as both checkpoints and 'celebration' points along the way. You should also have milestones where two or more tracks meet.

- Once you have your milestones in order of sequence, you have your project outline.

- The action steps are the individual actions required to achieve each milestone. The level of detail is up to you, but a good guide is to include any action which will take longer than an hour.

- You should estimate the length of time it will take to achieve each action step using your own experience, the experience of others involved in the project, the results of similar projects completed in the past and any relevant specialist advice.

- Committing to any timeline involves risk; you should always ensure that the degree of risk reflects the potential consequences. That is, be most pessimistic on critical actions.

- Add a contingency allowance of 10–20 per cent, depending on your experience.

- Complete the timeline backwards to determine the starting date.

- The critical path is the track containing the most urgent actions. That is, the track with the least amount of leeway (or 'slack time').

- Prepare contingency plans for any action where there is significant risk of failure and/or the consequences of failure would be serious. Consider a 'last resort' contingency for critical actions. When you brief your team on the main plan, brief them on the contingency plans also.

- Time spent now getting your timeline right will be repaid many times over once the project is under way: get it right first time.

3

CREATING AND MANAGING THE BUDGET

or Bean-counting for beginners

Columns of figures have a fascinating ability to divide the world into two types of people: those who cannot look at them without unconsciously checking the total for accuracy, and those who cannot look at them without falling asleep.

If you fall into the former category, you have no need of the system presented in this chapter. While the approach presented here was developed especially for this book and offers benefits to those new to financial management, it is based on a standard nine-column budget analysis sheet. You may, however, want to read my comments in the section entitled 'What is a budget? (1)', below.

If you fall into the latter category, take heart: so do I. The budget system presented in this chapter was designed specifically for the likes of you and me! The system is based on standard budgeting procedures, to satisfy your company accountant, but translates columns of figures into a colour-coded visual display system that makes it extremely easy to use.

A word of reassurance

If you ever feel the need to thoroughly confuse yourself, ask your company accountant to tell you the cost of producing any one of your company's products or services. You will quickly discover that an apparently simple term like 'cost' can be applied in dozens of different ways, and a simple question like 'how much does this item cost?' can sometimes result in a set of figures ranging from a few pence to thousands of pounds, depending on which particular definition of 'cost' you are using at the time.

That is the bad news. The good news is that this chapter does not attempt to delve into the murky depths of accountancy. It has one purpose, and one purpose alone: to enable you to produce a budget that will serve both you and your company accountant. You can achieve this without doing anything more complicated than operating an ordinary calculator (although you can use a computer spreadsheet, if you prefer), completing a simple form and referring to a colour-coded wall chart to let you know at a glance how the project is going.

What is a budget? (1)

Insanity is doing the same thing over and over again, expecting a different result.

Rita Mae Brown

Budgets, like costs, can be defined in many different ways. I want to preface my own definition with a few words of explanation.

Let us start by looking at how budgets work in an ideal world. In this ideal world, an independent team carries out an objective analysis of both the likely costs of the project, and the value of the intended benefits. This process is known, logically enough, as a cost-benefit analysis. If the anticipated value of the benefits is greater than the anticipated costs of the project, the scheme will be given the go-ahead; if not, it will be shelved. For example, if a marketing campaign is expected to bring in an additional £500 000 in profits and will cost £350 000 to implement, it would be given the go-ahead; if it will bring in an extra £500 000 profit but cost £525 000 to implement, it would be shelved as uneconomic (unless there are further benefits which justify the £25 000 net loss).

If the project does go ahead, the relationship between the forecast budget and the actual expenditure will be treated merely as useful information. Any significant discrepancy – whether above or below the forecast budget – will signify that something unexpected has happened. The unexpected event will be investigated to determine whether or not the budget is still an accurate forecast. If not, it will be adjusted accordingly and a new assessment made as to whether the project remains economic.

The real world, unfortunately, does not often work this way. The individual or team responsible for preparing the initial cost-benefit analysis will almost certainly not be independent. Most projects start because somebody wants them to, rather than simply in response to an identified need. It may be that the individual responsible wants the project to be given the go-ahead for perfectly genuine reasons: he or she honestly believes that it will benefit the organization. It is equally possible that they have more personal reasons: a desire to work in a particular field, the kudos of an important project or an interest in using the extra resources the project will attract to satisfy empire-building ambitions. Whatever his or her motives, however, the project proposer is in no position to prepare a totally objective cost-benefit analysis – being the person who actively wants the project to be given the green light. Yet it is often he or she who will be responsible for performing the cost-benefit analysis as part of the project proposal.

Whether deliberately or subconsciously, the project proposer – who will have spent a considerable amount of time in preparing his or her case – may tend to exaggerate the benefits and underplay the costs.

The personality of the project proposer and culture of the organization may also introduce inaccuracies. Some individuals – and organizations – apply a kind of 'negative contingency allowance' to the costs of a project ('Well, the supplier has quoted £10 000 but we can probably beat them down to £8 000 – stick it in at £8 000').

A major consideration is the inertia generated by a project: once it is under way, it tends to keep going even if costs rise beyond all recognition. Many organizations are almost obsessively reluctant to cut their losses on an ailing project, even when it is clear to any independent observer that the cheapest action would be either to abandon the project altogether or start again with a totally different approach. This tendency is compounded by the attitudes of banks and other financiers – it may be safer for the organization to continue with a hopeless project while telling the banks that things will be allright – all the while hoping for a miracle in some other aspect of the business – than to admit that the money spent so far has been wasted and risk the bank pulling the plug.

Some project proposers will use this phenomenon to their advantage, deliberately quoting unrealistic costings in an attempt to get the project off the ground, secure in the knowledge that extra funds will almost certainly be made available when it becomes apparent that the true costs are higher than forecast.

It is also possible to fall into the opposite trap. Some organizations enforce budgets rigorously, expecting project managers to get it right to the penny. This encourages a 'think of a number and double it' approach: project managers grossly overestimate the anticipated costs in order to give themselves breathing space, and to earn brownie points when they bring the project home under budget.

In neither case can the resulting forecast be described as a budget. And both have high costs to the organization. Where costs are underestimated, the organization is likely to waste money on projects that should never have been undertaken in the first place. Where costs are overestimated, wasted expenditure can almost be guaranteed.

If you are the project proposer, you will have to make your own decision as to whether or not to engage in the kind of politics described. If you decide that you cannot avoid such games, at least ensure that you have an accurate forecast for your own personal use.

If the budget is assigned for you, use the approach presented in this chapter to prepare your own, independent budget. If you are the one responsible for completing the project within budget, you need to be confident that the budget offered is a realistic one.

What is a budget? (2)

My own definition of a realistic and useful budget (divorced from politics and games playing) would be: *a means of ensuring that you have sufficient resources to complete the project, and of monitoring the continued feasibility of the project as it is carried out.*

It is clear that the budget needs to satisfy two criteria. First, it must provide a realistic forecast of the likely expenditure before you begin. Second, it must provide ongoing information on whether or not the project is running to budget, and if not why not, once it is under way.

Calculating the benefits

The starting point for any project budget is to calculate the value of the benefits you expect to generate. In some cases, this may be relatively straightforward. A sales promotion is clearly intended to generate increased sales and therefore increased profits. An investment in some form of automation is normally designed to reduce operating costs. In these cases, you would call on the experience of similar past projects to estimate the likely value of the anticipated benefits.

In other cases, such as a staff incentive scheme, it may be far more difficult to estimate the likely value of the benefits to the organization, particularly if the project is the first of its kind. Get as much information and expert advice as you can, but do not worry about getting the estimate correct to the penny: all estimates are, by their very nature, simply educated guesses. We try to make them as educated as possible, but even the chairmen of multinationals sometimes get it impressively wrong. In the very first days of computing, for example, the then chairman of IBM predicted that the total, world-wide market for computers would be unlikely to exceed five machines . . .

Remember to factor in to the equation non-monetary benefits like improved staff satisfaction. When it has been estimated that the true cost of losing a middle manager to a competitor may well be over £100 000 – sometimes very much more – the so-called 'soft' factors have hard financial worth. Similarly, if a project will save staff time, the value may be much greater than you would expect. Your accounts department will be able to place a financial value on a surprising number of factors!

Once you have an all-in estimate of the benefits of the project, you are ready to calculate the costs.

Preparing a master budget form

The first stage of calculating the costs is to prepare a budget form. This form will list every single item of anticipated expenditure and record both forecast and actual expenditure.

Where the actual expenditure is higher or lower than expected, your budget form will reveal the reason for this. There are only three ways a project can go over budget: you can buy something you did not expect to buy, you can buy more of something than you expected or you can pay a higher price than you expected. Your budget form will tell you which of these was responsible, and show you the difference between anticipated and actual cost in both percentage and cash terms.

You will probably use a large number of these forms – prepare one, then make plenty of photocopies. Alternatively, if you are familiar with a computer spreadsheet, use this instead – it will make life easier by doing the calculations for you.

Whether you are using paper forms or a spreadsheet, the format is the same. You need an A4 sheet. Turn it on its side so that it is wider than it is deep (if using a spreadsheet, select Landscape in the page setup routine). Divide it into 11 columns as shown in Figure 3.1. Then label the columns as in Figure 3.2.

Alternatively, if you have a photocopier with a zoom enlargement facility, you may be able simply to copy the form in Figure 3.2 and enlarge it to A4 size.

The meaning of each column is explained below (do not worry if you are not entirely sure about all the terms at this stage – we will work through an example shortly).

Item
This is simply a unique code for each item of expenditure. You can use a simple numerical sequence like 0001, 0002, 0003, etc., or you can use part numbers, reference codes or whatever you like. The important thing is that each item should have a unique code; this will allow you to refer to it in shorthand without rewriting the full name each time.

Description
The full name of the item. This should also specify the units you will be using. For example, 'Widgets (box of 10)' or 'Middle manager (one day of time)'

Qty (E)
The quantity of the item you *expect* to need. Since the description column already specifies the units, the quantity column need contain only a number.

Unit cost (E)
The *expected* price or cost per item. Again, this figure refers to the unit specified in the Description column.

Total cost (E)
The expected total cost of this item. That is, Qty (E) x Unit cost (E).

Figure 3.1 A blank master budget form

Item	Description	ESTIMATE			ACTUAL			VARIANCE		
		Qty (E)	Unit cost (E)	Total cost (E)	Qty (A)	Unit cost (A)	Total cost (A)	Qty (D)	Cost (D) %	Cost (D) £

Figure 3.2 Column headings for the master budget form

Qty (A)   The quantity of the item you *actually* use.

Unit cost (A)   The *actual* cost of each item.

Total cost (A)   The *actual* total cost of this item. That is, Qty (A) x Unit cost (A).

Qty (D) %   The *difference* between the quantity you expected to use, and the quantity you actually used. That is, Qty (A) - Qty (E) calculated as a percentage. This may be either positive (meaning you used more than expected) or negative (meaning you used less). For example, if you actually used 120 units and expected to use 100 units, the difference is +20 per cent. If you actually used only 75 units when you expected to use 100, the difference is -25 per cent.

Cost (D) %   The *difference* between the total amount you expected the item to cost, and the total amount it actually did cost. That is, Total cost (A) - Total cost (E), again calculated as a percentage.

Cost (D) £   The *difference* between the total amount you expected the item to cost, and the total amount it actually did cost. That is, Total cost (A) - Total cost (E), this time just left in pounds rather than turned into a percentage.

Let us take an example to see how this would work in practice.

A sample entry on the budget form

Your project requires some industrial quality widgets. This is the first item of expenditure in your budget, so you put 0001 into the Item column. You then put the description, 'Industrial Widgets', into the Description column. You expect to need 10 of them, so you enter 10 in the Qty (E) column.

Your supplier tells you widgets cost £100 each, so you put £100 into the Unit Cost (E) column. You multiply the quantity by the price to get £1000, so enter £1000 in the Total Cost (E) column:

Once the project is under way, however, and the time comes to buy the widgets, you find that you need 15 of them, rather than 10. When you phone your supplier, you find that ordering 15 units instead of 10 entitles you to a 10 per cent discount, so the widgets will cost you £90 each instead of £100. You thus put 15 in the Qty (A) column and £90 in the Unit Cost (A) column. You multiply the actual quantity by the actual price to arrive at £1350, so enter £1350 in the Total Cost (A) column.

You now calculate the difference in quantity between the 10 you expected to buy, and the 15 you actually bought, *as a percentage*. This is done by dividing the quantity you bought (the figure in the Qty (A) column) by the quantity you expected to buy (the figure in the Qty (E) column), multiplying by 100 and then subtracting 100 from the total. In our example, $15 \div 10 = 1.5$. Next, $1.5 \times 100 = 150$. Finally, $150 - 100 = 50$. The percentage difference in quantity is thus 50. So we enter '+50%' in the Qty (D) column.

You now perform exactly the same calculation on the difference in cost. That is, we divide the actual total cost (the figure in the Total Cost (A) column) by the expected total cost (the figure in the Total Cost (E) column), multiply by 100 and then subtract 100 from the total. In our example, $1350 \div 1000 = 1.35$. Next, $1.35 \times 100 = 135$. Finally, $135 - 100 = 35$. The percentage difference in cost is thus 35. So we enter '+35%' in the Total Cost (D) column.

Finally, subtract the total amount the item actually cost (the figure in the column Total Cost (A)) from the total amount you expected it to cost (the figure in column Total Cost (E)) to get the actual difference between the budgeted expenditure and the actual expenditure. In this example, you expected to pay £1000 and actually paid £1350. So £1350 – £1000 = £350 and we enter '+£350' in the Cost (D) £ column. Figure 3.3 shows the completed form.

The budget form in Figure 3.4 shows a few more examples, with the calculations already done.

Filling in the budget form

Run through your timeline, one action at a time, and think about what costs will be incurred in completing each action. Again, use your own experience, advice from colleagues, past budgets and specialist advice to guide you.

Ask your company accountant about how to account for 'standard'

Item	Description	ESTIMATE			ACTUAL			VARIANCE		
		Qty (E)	Unit cost (E)	Total cost (E)	Qty (A)	Unit cost (A)	Total cost (A)	Qty (D)	Cost (D) %	Cost (D) £
0001	Indust. widgets	10	£100.00	£1000.00	15	£90.00	£1350.00	+50%	+35%	+£350

Figure 3.3 A sample entry

Item	Description	ESTIMATE			ACTUAL			VARIANCE		
		Qty (E)	Unit cost (E)	Total cost (E)	Qty (A)	Unit cost (A)	Total cost (A)	Qty (D)	Cost (D) %	Cost (D) £
0001	Indust. widgets	10	£100.00	£1000.00	15	£90.00	£1350.00	+50%	+35%	+£350
0002	Widget joints	10	£10.00	£100.00	12	£11.00	£132.00	+20%	+10%	+£32
0003	Paint (litres)	5	£2.00	£10.00	5	£2.00	£10.00	–	–	–
0004	Tacks (box 50)	100	£1.00	£100.00	100	£1.25	£125.00	–	+25%	+£25
0005	Brackets	50	£4.00	£200.00	25	£4.00	£100.00	–50%	0%	–£100

Figure 3.4 More sample entries

expenditure like phone calls and travel – these are often lumped together in a single item and calculated as a percentage of your organization's total overhead.

Enter each item onto your master budget form. At this stage, you will simply complete the first five columns: Item, Description, Qty (E), Unit Cost (E), and Total Cost (E). The remaining columns will be completed when you come to actually buy the items.

Remember to cost in the value of staff time. A project which seems very inexpensive can turn out to be totally uneconomic once you have costed the time of all the staff required to implement it. Staff costs are an essential factor to include if you are deciding whether to complete a project in-house or use an outside company. Again, your accounts department will advise you on how to account for staff costs, but as a rule of thumb, the total cost to an organization of a junior member of staff (salary plus employers' national insurance, expenses, etc.) is one-and-a-half times that person's salary; for a senior manager, the cost is around twice the salary (allowing for more expensive pensions, company car, secretary, larger office and so on).

When preparing your budget, you need to find a balance between costing every single item to the penny – a process which would almost certainly be an uneconomic use of your time – and wild guesses. Aim to be as accurate as you can, but do not spend hours trying to work out whether something will cost £1000 or £1200. Reliable estimates are a perfectly normal part of any budget, and nobody will thank you for spending £100 worth of your own time trying to work out if you can save £50.

Preparing a budget timeline

The total cost of your budget, obtained by totalling the Total Cost (E) column, is only half the story. It tells you the total estimated cost of the project, and will afterwards reveal whether or not you met your budget, but does not give any clue as to how you are doing *during* the project. This is where our budget timeline comes in.

The budget timeline will tell you literally at a glance whether or not you are within budget *at any given point in the project*. If you are beyond your budget, it will show where this happened and whether or not you are still within your overall contingency allowance. You can thus instantly tell whether or not you need to take urgent action to correct the problem.

Photocopy the budget timeline form given in Figure 3.5 (you may want to use a copier with an enlargement facility to copy it onto A4 paper):

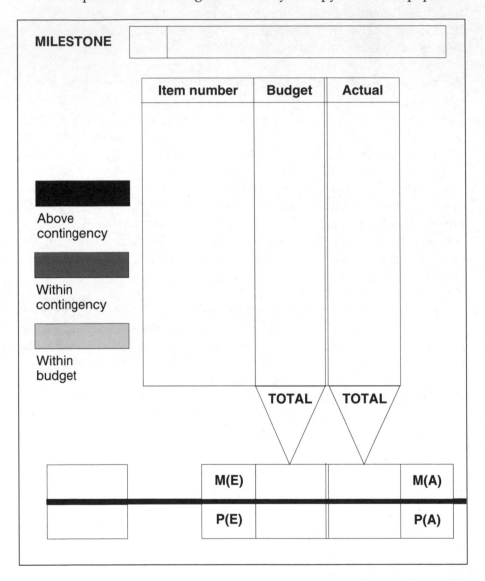

Figure 3.5 A blank budget timeline form

You will need one of these sheets for every milestone in your project, so you will again want to make plenty of copies. You should also use coloured stickers to turn the grey shading into (from top to bottom) red, orange and green.

Start with your first milestone. Write the name of the milestone at the top of the sheet, and number the sheet. Next, enter the Item number (from the Item column of your master budget form) of each expense you will incur in reaching this milestone. For each one, enter the Total Cost (E) figure in the Budget column. Leave the Actual column blank.

For example, suppose that your first milestone was called Widgets painted. You would enter 'Widgets painted' in the space at the top of the sheet, and number the sheet 1.

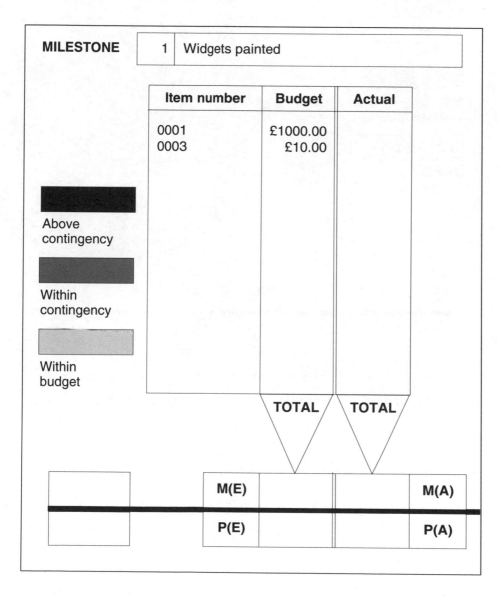

Figure 3.6 A sample entry

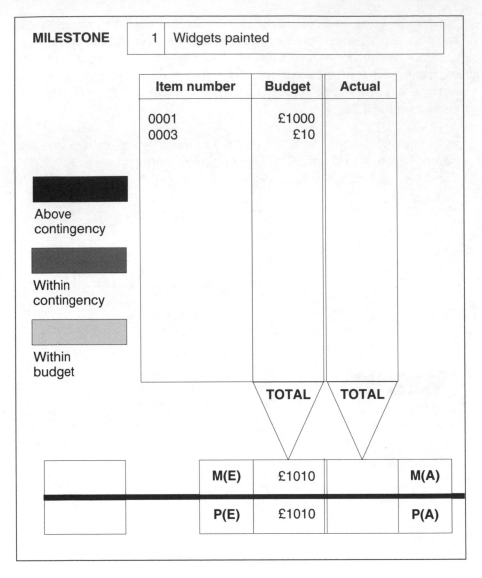

Figure 3.7 Adding the estimated costs of the milestone and the project to date

Now assume that to achieve this milestone, you have to buy the widgets (item 0001) and the paint (item 0003). You enter '0001' in the Item column. Next you look in the Total Cost (E) column of the master budget form to find that the expected cost is £1 000. You put this amount in the Budget column of the timeline, and do exactly the same for the paint as shown in Figure 3.6.

(For simplicity's sake, I suggest that you work to the nearest pound on your timeline, reserving the exact figures for your master budget form.) The total expected cost of achieving this milestone is thus £1 010. You write this figure in the M(E) box – Milestone (estimated).

In the P(E) – Project (Estimated) – box, you write the expected *total cost of the project so far*. Since this is the first milestone of the project, it is the same as the figure in the M(E) box as illustrated in Figure 3.7.

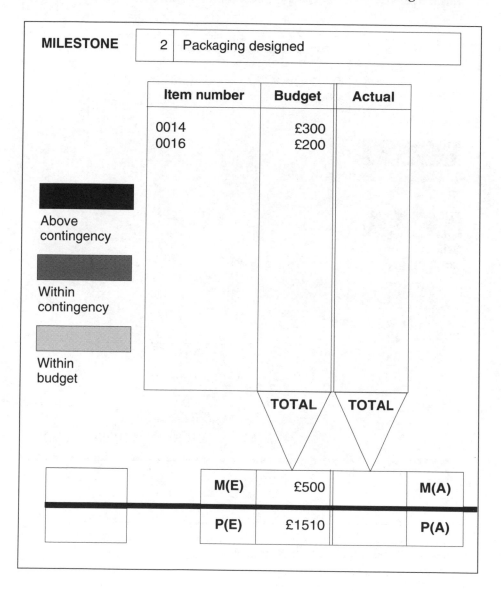

Figure 3.8 The budget timeline entry for the second milestone

Now take a new sheet and do the same thing for the next milestone. However, this time, you calculate the P(E) figure – the total expected cost of the project so far – by adding the M(E) figure to the previous sheet's P(E) figure. This is obvious if you think about it – the total expected cost of the project so far is the previous expected cost plus the expected cost of the new milestone.

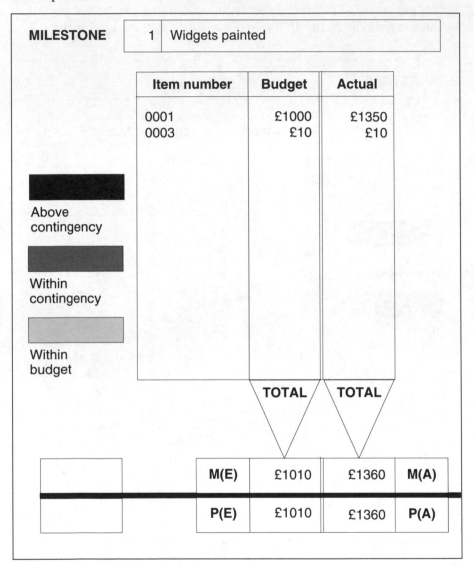

Figure 3.9 Updating the budget timeline

For example, if our second milestone had a total expected cost of £500, the new total expected project cost so far is £1010 + £500 = £1510 as in Figure 3.8.

Continue this process for each milestone. You will now see exactly when you expect to spend each part of your budget, and how the total cost will mount up.

Once you have completed the budget timeline, stick the sheets in sequence on to a roll of paper and stick it up on your wall underneath your main timeline.

Once the project is under way, you can complete the 'actual' column of your timeline by simply transferring the figures from your master budget form. For example, we said earlier that you expected to buy 10 widgets at a cost of £100 each, but actually bought 15 at a cost of £90 each. The entry in our master budget form looked like the example shown in Figure 3.3 (see page 45).

Simply copy the figure from the Total cost (A) column to the Actual column of your budget timeline sheet. Do the same for all the items on that sheet, and enter the total actual cost of achieving that milestone in the M(A) box as shown in Figure 3.9.

Add the figure in the M(A) box to the figure in the previous sheet's P(A) box, and you have the updated actual cost of the project to date.

Adding unexpected costs

If you buy something you did not allow for, add this item to the end of your master budget form. Put a zero in the Qty (E), Unit Cost (E) and Total Cost (E) columns, leave the Qty (D) % and Total Cost (D) % columns blank and put the same figure in the Total Cost (D) £ as you have in the Total Cost (A) column.

Colour coding the timeline

We claimed earlier that this system would provide an at-a-glance method of seeing whether or not you are within budget and, if not, why not. This is achieved by colour coding each sheet of the budget timeline.

You may have wondered about the purpose of the two blank boxes at the bottom-left of the sheet. These will be used for the colour-coding. The colour coding system is as follows:

Green	Within budget
Orange	Over budget but within your contingency allowance
Red	Over budget and beyond your contingency allowance

If *the current milestone* was achieved within budget, colour the top box green. If it was over budget but within your overall contingency allowance (let's say you allowed 20 per cent contingency and the milestone cost 12 per cent more than expected), colour it orange. And if it was over budget and beyond your contingency allowance, colour it red.

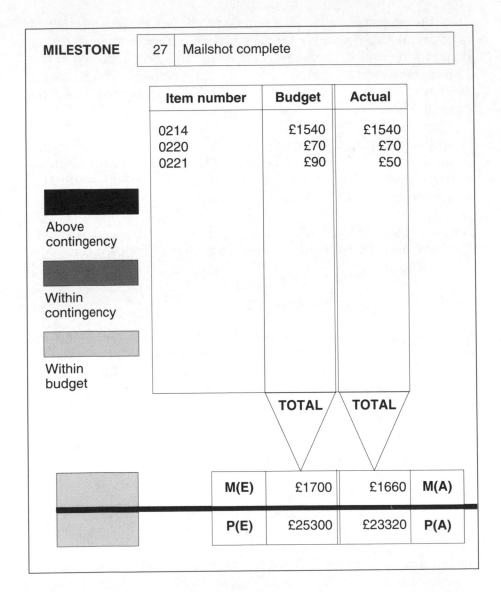

Figure 3.10(a) Colour coding the budget timeline

Now, apply the same colour coding to the bottom box, but this time referring to *the whole project to date* instead of just the current milestone.

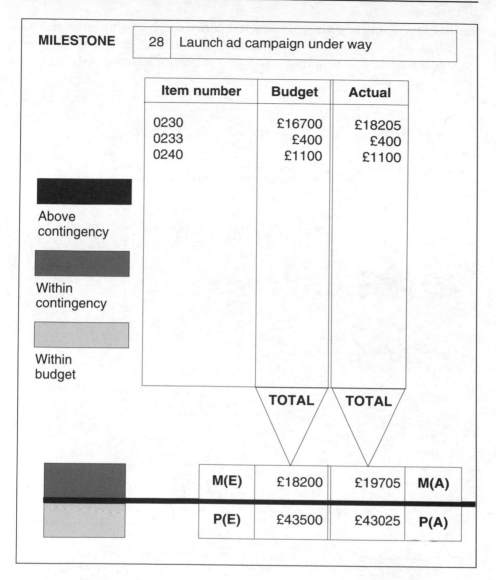

MILESTONE	28	Launch ad campaign under way

Item number	Budget	Actual
0230	£16700	£18205
0233	£400	£400
0240	£1100	£1100

Above contingency

Within contingency

Within budget

	TOTAL	TOTAL	
M(E)	£18200	£19705	M(A)
P(E)	£43500	£43025	P(A)

Figure 3.10(b) Colour coding the budget timeline

How might this look in practice? Since this book does not have colour, light shading has been used for green, medium shading for orange and dark shading for red. In the first sheet, Figure 3.10(a), the current milestone was achieved within budget, so both boxes are coloured green – nothing to worry about here.

In the second sheet, Figure 3.10(b), the milestone went over budget but by less than your 20 per cent contingency allowance, so the top box is coloured orange. The project as a whole is still on budget, however, so the bottom box is still coloured green. This is a warning sign, that something unexpected happened with this milestone. You would want to look at the milestone to find out why it went over budget, and check whether the same factor might apply to any of your future milestones.

MILESTONE	29	Press and dealer launches done

Item number	Budget	Actual
0241	£7900	£11500
0242	£1600	£2100
0244	£4200	£4200

Above contingency

Within contingency

Within budget

	TOTAL	TOTAL	
M(E)	£13700	£17800	M(A)
P(E)	£57200	£60825	P(A)

Figure 3.10(c) Colour coding the budget timeline

In the third sheet, Figure 3.10(c), the milestone went way over budget – by more than your 20 per cent contingency allowance – so the top box is coloured red. This is a danger sign, indicating that something very unexpected happened with this milestone. You would want to look very carefully indeed at how it happened, and to find out whether the same factor might affect future milestones. The extra expense on this milestone means that the project as a whole is now over budget, although still within your 20 per cent contingency allowance, so the bottom box is coloured orange. This indicates that it is urgent that you identify the problem in all your orange and red milestones.

Obviously, if the project as a whole goes beyond your contingency allowance, and thus the bottom box is coloured red, it is critical that you identify and correct the problem.

You can see that the colour-coding system fulfils its promise: you can see at a glance how the project as a whole is going from the colour of the lower boxes, and tell *where* it went wrong by checking the colour of the upper boxes. Referring to the master budget form will provide the detailed figures illustrating the root cause of the problem – either spending money on things that you did not budget for, buying more of something than you expected or paying a higher price than expected.

Do not ignore items which go over-budget, even if the project as a whole is still on track. Always find out how it happened, in case it is likely to happen again later in the project. If you have reason to suspect that your budget is no longer reliable, stop and redo the budget.

Recalculating the budget

Again, you need to find the right balance. No project ever runs precisely to budget, and if you recalculated your budget every time something went a little over, you would not have time to work on the project itself. On the other hand, it is important that you follow up any significant errors. If your budget is held on a computer spreadsheet, recalculating costs is very much easier and can therefore be done more frequently.

Identifying the significant errors in a budget is where the final three columns of your master budget form come into play. Develop the habit of scanning down these last three columns. Look for any percentage figure above your contingency allowance, and any pound figure above a certain threshold. The threshold will depend on the total cost of the project – an extra £500 will not be particularly alarming in a £100 000 project, but would be extremely serious in a £2 000 project.

Whenever you decide that it is necessary to recalculate, make sure that you clearly label the revised budget with a version number and date, and that everyone involved is given the most up-to-date version. This may sound obvious, but it is not unknown for an organization to discover too late that it is working to the wrong version of a budget.

When recalculating, use your experience and not your prayers! When a project is running over budget, it can be tempting to try to balance things out by making optimistic assumptions about the future. Remember that you are already over budget precisely because your *original* budget turned out to be optimistic – if anything, you need to be more pessimistic now.

Look at trends, not just the latest figures. For example, if you expected to need 10 widgets a month, and you actually needed 15 in the first month and 20 in the second, you may need 25 next month with a similar rise in each successive month.

Finally, once you have recalculated your budget, go back to the original cost-benefit analysis. Is the project still worthwhile? And is your planned approach still the best one? A common error is to continue with an in-house project in the face of rapidly rising costs, when it is in fact cheaper to hire an outside company who can be commissioned to do the job for a fixed fee. Once the contract has been signed, any unexpected surprises become the contractor's problem. *However*, do not try to hide anything from the contractor – this simply guarantees that the project will grind to a halt at some point amid bitter wranglings.

SUMMARY

- You do not have to be an accounting expert to create and manage a budget.

- Budgets are often based more on organizational politics than on accurate forecasting; if you have to indulge in such games, always create an accurate forecast for your own use.

- A budget is 'a means of ensuring that you have sufficient resources to complete the project and of monitoring the continued feasibility of the project as it is carried out'.

- To satisfy this definition, a budget must provide a realistic forecast of the likely expenditure before you begin, and it must provide ongoing information on whether or not the project is running to budget (and if not, why not) once it is under way. The system described in this chapter satisfies these criteria.

- The starting point for evaluating the feasibility of any project is to compare the anticipated value of the benefits with the anticipated costs; when calculating the value of benefits, remember to cost-in the so-called 'soft' factors like job satisfaction – these usually have hard financial worth.

- An important part of the cost of any project will be the cost of staff time. As a rule of thumb, a junior member of staff should be costed at one-and-a-half times salary while a senior manager should be costed at twice their salary.

- When preparing the budget, strike a balance between costing every item to the penny (a process which would cost more than it could save) and wild guesses. Educated guesses for low-cost items are an accepted part of any budget.

- Keep your budget up to date. Update it daily or weekly, depending on the size of the project. If something goes over budget, ask yourself whether this has implications for the future. If necessary, recalculate the project and then re-examine whether the project is still economic.

- If you do need to recalculate, base the revised budget on your experience not your prayers! If you are over budget, be more pessimistic with the revised one – do not compound the error in a vain attempt to balance the books.

- When recalculating, examine trends as well as the latest figures. If costs have risen, will they rise further during the life of the project?

- When you have your revised budget, go back to your cost-benefit analysis – is the project still worthwhile, and is your planned approach still the best one? Or would you be better off scrapping your work and starting again, perhaps using an outside contractor?

- If you do use a contractor, negotiate a fixed fee for the job, but *don't* hide any material facts – this simply guarantees that the project will grind to a messy halt.

4

CREATING PROJECT MAPS

or Job satisfaction is not an optional extra

In Hollywood disaster movies, there is usually a grizzled project manager charged with the job of saving the Earth from impending destruction. Every piece of sophisticated equipment is made available at a moment's notice, teams of people scurry about ready to obey his (it is invariably a he) every command, and the most foreboding obstacles are swept aside with a few barked orders. Within 90 minutes, our conquering hero emerges to the rapturous applause of the thronging crowds and a quiet word of congratulation from the President. The project manager shrugs, allows a little smile of satisfaction to flicker briefly across his face, mutters that it was nothing and walks off into the setting sun with a wide-eyed girl on his arm.

If this sounds like a fair description of your working life, you have no need of this chapter. Some of you, however, may find that your situation differs from this image in a few minor details. The project objective, however worthwhile, is not always romantic. The resources available to you may appear inadequate. Your team may be rather thin on the ground. Obstacles can appear insurmountable. And you may find that support and appreciation for your work is not always apparent.

None of the above need apply at the beginning of the project. Most of us embark on a new project with an abundance of energy and enthusiasm (if you don't, it may be worth skipping ahead to take a look at Chapter 8). But this initial burst of energy and enthusiasm is not enough to sustain you throughout a lengthy project. You need some means of ensuring that both you and your team *remain* inspired, even when the going gets tough. And you need to plan for this *now*, while your enthusiasm is at its peak.

When it comes to being inspired, there is no substitute for success. When everything is going well, and everyone is confident that the project is on track, inspiration is not usually a problem. The problems start when the project seems stuck, when there is no visible progress. Unfortunately, there are times during every project when your progress may not seem apparent.

Any sales manager will tell you that it takes a certain number of rejections for every successful sale, and that each rejection takes you closer to a sale. Yet, at the time, a rejection does not look like progress. The same principle applies to any project: there are certain actions you need to take that are necessary, yet do not seem to bring you any closer to your objective. Even if you fail in a particular approach, you have now eliminated an approach that does not work and are that much closer to developing an approach that *will* work. Project maps are a simple but effective means of reassuring yourself and your team that you are making headway, even when you do not appear to be producing results.

What is a project map?

> It is good to have an end to journey towards, but it is the journey that matters in the end.
>
> Ursula Le Guin

A project map is a visual record of progress. More specifically, it measures the 'intangibles' – factors that are typically ignored or overlooked in the quest for hard results but nonetheless contribute to getting the job done.

A sales project provides a good example. On average, a widget sales executive may have to make 25 calls for every successful sale. That is, for every 25 calls he or she makes, 24 people will not be interested. Experienced sales executives quickly become familiar with the statistics, and are no longer deterred by the rejections. They mentally or literally tick off the rejection and view each 'no' as narrowing the odds on the next call being successful.

Those new to sales will inevitably take a more limited view. As far as they are concerned, their job is to sell widgets and a rejection is a failure. The first rejection is a disappointment, the second a bigger disappointment, the tenth one clearly means that they are failing and the twentieth rejection may be enough to convince them that they are in the wrong job. They never go on to reach that twenty-fifth call.

While this example may sound silly viewed from the outside, it is more common than you would expect. A similar process can occur in almost any type of project. If you are responsible for finding a conference venue, for example, you might think that you are not making progress after viewing and rejecting as unsuitable 15 possible sites. Yet, viewed from the outside, this is clearly nonsense: the main action required to identify a conference venue is to visit possible venues, and you have made a great deal of progress in this. Not only that, but you probably have a much clearer idea of your requirements than when you started.

Project maps are designed to illustrate clearly progress which might otherwise be overlooked or discounted.

Types of project map

There is no fixed format for a project map, but three criteria can be applied.

1. It must inspire you and your team into action. It must make you actively want to get on with the project in order to see visible progress on the map. This means that everyone on the team must instantly be able to make sense of the map, and that it must be prominently displayed on an office wall or noticeboard.

2. It must measure factors over which you have direct control, not just end results. In our sales example, you do *not* have direct control over the number of sales you make. You *do* have direct control over, for example, the number of prospecting calls you make. It is fine to include both – you will normally want to see the results of your endeavours, after all – but always ensure that you include factors that you can directly control.

3. The units of measurement must be small enough to allow you to record progress every single day. (I will come back to this point in a moment, after you have looked at some typical project maps.)

The simplest form of project map is to break your milestone down into factors over which you have control. For a conference, measure things like the number of possible conference venues visited, the number of people added to the invitation list and the number of potential speakers identified. For sales projects, measure calls made, brochures sent out, clients visited; similarly for charity fundraising projects. For market research projects, measure the number of people you have spoken to, and keep a separate measurement of people who turn out not to be qualified for the survey – eliminating them still represents progress. And so on. An exhaustive list is beyond the scope of this book, but always apply the three tests given above.

Once you have chosen the factors you will measure, you can create a simple bar chart. For example, for a sales project see Figure 4.1. If you know the statistics relating to your job, for example that it takes 25 calls to make a sale, you can plot these side by side as in Figure 4.2. This will reveal whether or not you are on track.

Calls made	Brochures sent out	Appointments made	Sales
200	200	20	20
190	190	19	19
180	180	18	18
170	170	17	17
160	160	16	16
150	150	15	15
140	140	14	14
130	130	13	13
120	120	12	12
110	110	11	11
100	100	10	10
90	90	9	9
80	80	8	8
70	70	7	7
60	60	6	6
50	50	5	5
40	40	4	4
30	30	3	3
20	20	2	2
10	10	1	1

Figure 4.1 An example of a project map for a sales project

Where numbers cannot easily be used to measure progress, you can simply break each milestone down into its component actions. Make sure, however, that you include each individual action so that all progress is visible. A useful format for this type of project map is shown by Figure 4.3.

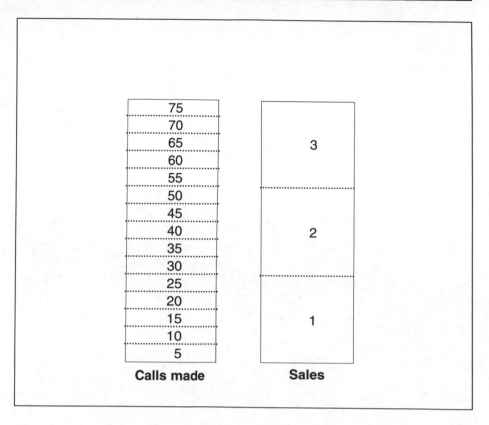

Figure 4.2 A more sophisticated project map for a sales project

Remember, however, the third criterion – that the unit of measurement is small enough to allow you to record progress every day. If an individual action will take longer than a day, break it up into several separate actions. For example, if 'Design customer survey form' will take three days, break it up into something like 'Gather input on questions from each department'; 'Collate questions'; 'Produce draft survey form'; 'Invite feedback' and 'Pass final form to marketing'.

A project map, unlike a timeline, does not need to provide you with an overview of the entire project. Its sole purpose is to illustrate current progress. You can thus have different project maps for different phases of the project and display only the current map. The different maps do not need to be consistent – so long as everyone involved can easily understand them you can use as many different formats as you like.

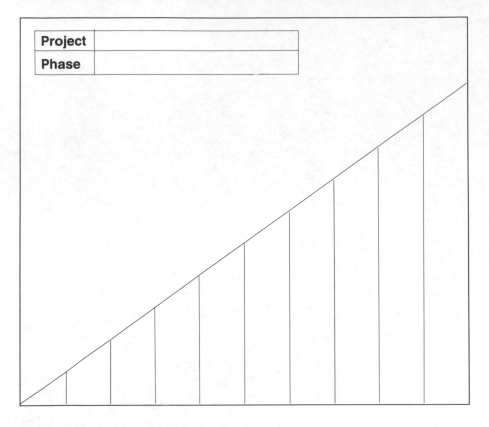

Figure 4.3 A universal project map

Three-dimensional project maps

Project maps need not be two-dimensional; you can use physical objects as well as diagrams. You could place coloured pins on a map, representing calls made, brochures sent, customer sites, venues inspected, delegates booked and so on. You can use toys to represent products – for example toy cars of different colours to represent test drives performed and cars sold. Photos can be effective – for example, photos of VIPs who have accepted an invitation to an event, photos of countries in which you have sales representatives and so on. You can use almost anything as units of measurement: marbles, coins, coloured magnets and so on. You can even fill perspex tubes with dyed water! Do not be afraid to be 'silly'; some of the project maps used in a sales environment can appear ridiculous, but they produce results. It is at times when everyone is feeling very serious about the whole thing that a little humour can make an enormous difference.

Computer graphics

You can also use computer-generated graphics, but these have the same drawback as computerized project management software: to be effective, a project map has to be displayed on a wall or noticeboard where everyone can see them. If the software is too fiddly, or takes too long to print, it will not be instantly updated, thus defeating the object.

Also, project maps usually look much more effective in colour. Colour printers are now available, though not yet common.

Finally, you may want to make it possible for *anyone* to update a project map so that when somebody makes some progress they mark that progress on the map themselves. This is not usually practical if the map is stored on a computer system.

Practicality

There are some occasions when a project map can be both inspirational *and* practical. A good example is a map of delegates booked for a conference. While the conference registrar will have the details in his or her filing system, it is also useful if the total numbers are clearly visible on a project map for all to see. This can dramatically reduce the time people spend trying to track down information: a single wall-chart can provide the information needed for everything from seating plans to notepad supplies and catering arrangements.

There is a danger here though, that practical considerations will take over. If a project map becomes overburdened with detail, or starts looking more like a spreadsheet than a colourful chart, consider designing two separate maps: one for practical information, and the other for inspiration.

SUMMARY

- Most of us begin new projects with energy and enthusiasm, but while this is enough at the outset, it will not sustain you through a lengthy project once the novelty has worn off.

- There are times during every project when nothing much seems to be happening, when progress seems slow or non-existent. It is during these times that results-orientated measurements become depressing rather then inspiring; something more is needed.

- Project maps are visual records of progress. Specifically, they measure the 'intangible' progress which is often overlooked or ignored, but nevertheless contributes to getting the job done.

- There is no fixed format for a project map. It must, however, satisfy three criteria. First, it must inspire you and your team into action, especially when the going gets tough. If it fails this test, it doesn't matter how pretty it is, it does not work. Second, it must measure factors over which you have direct control, and not just measure results. Third, the units of measurement chosen must be small enough to allow you to record progress every single day.

- The simplest method of producing a project map is to break your milestones down into factors over which you have direct control – potential venues visited, people added to the invitation list, potential speakers identified and so on.

- If you have a good idea of the statistics of a task (for example, that you have to visit an average of 15 sites to confirm a suitable conference venue), you can plot the actions (visiting sites) against the result (confirming a venue) graphically to illustrate that 15 site visits should add up to one venue confirmed.

- Where numbers cannot easily be used to measure progress, simply break down each milestone into its individual component actions and plot these using the triangular chart illustrated by Figure 4.3. If an action will take longer than a day, break it up into sub-actions – even artificially if necessary (for example – survey form 25% complete, 50% complete, 75% complete and 100% complete).

- Project maps do not have to be two-dimensional: you can use physical objects as well as diagrams: coloured pins on a map, photos, toys, marbles, coins, coloured magnets and so on. Don't be afraid of silly' maps – humour is the best way of helping people keep a sense of perspective when time is short.

- Computer graphics can create impressive project maps, but use them with care – to work, project maps must be easy to update by everyone involved in the project. If the software is too complex, or it takes too long to print, people will not update it.

- Project maps can often be practical as well as inspirational, providing an at-a-glance guide to the status of a task or project, but remember that the point of the map is to inspire action; if they become overburdened with detail, or look too serious, consider designing two maps – one for practicalities and one for inspiration.

5

CREATING A WINNING TEAM

or Leave the lone hero stuff to the cowboys

Name the second man to set foot on the moon, and five of the senior managers behind the manned lunar landing programme. No? How about the second man to reach the summit of Everest, and the four most important members of the team that made the ascent possible? Still no? Well then, what about the names of the coaches of any five Olympic Gold Medallists? No idea? Try the names of any three of the behind-the-scenes organizers of the Live Aid concert. Still no luck?

If you look at virtually any of our planet's celebrated achievements, it quickly becomes evident that we have been raised on the romantic myth that these impressive feats are the work of single individuals. We see only the person in the spotlight, not the often vast teams of people required to make the achievement possible.

This myth is a dangerous one for project managers. It instils in us the idea that we should be able to complete vast projects single-handedly, with others playing only a minor supporting role. It encourages the idea that we must do most of the work, while others merely help out here and there. In reality, nothing could be further from the truth, as anyone who has ever managed a large-scale project will quickly confirm. All the significant achievements in history – even those that are thought of as the works of a lone individual – were the works of teams. The manned lunar landing programme involved a team of thousands. The first successful Everest expedition consisted of a large team of both climbers and porters. Nobody wins an Olympic Gold Medal without a coach, fellow athletes to train with and the financial support of individuals, organizations or governments. The Live Aid concert was made possible by the work of thousands of volunteers around the world.

Every action is a form of communication

Change the way people think, and things will never be the same.
Steve Biko

The lone hero myth is doubly dangerous because it can lead us to view the project as somehow separate from the team that will achieve it. And yet, if you take a look through the actions on your timeline, you will quickly discover that nothing could be further from the truth: virtually every action listed is ultimately a form of communication.

Ordering goods or services? Communicating your needs to a supplier. Writing a progress report? A written communication to your manager(s). Writing a sales brochure? Communicating benefits to potential customers. Drawing up a schedule? Communicating anticipated dates to colleagues/suppliers/customers/managers/staff/yourself at a later date. Calculating costs? Communicating financial information to those who read your budget. Drafting a market research questionnaire? Requesting potential customers to communicate their needs to you. And so on.

Since achieving your objective is dependent on completing the actions on your timeline, and those actions rely on successful communication with the people involved, it makes sense to invest a little time in defining your team and clarifying the lines of communication within it.

Defining your team

At first glance, your team may appear to be a small one. It may even appear that you *are* the team. Yet, if you look at the actions on your timeline, the chances are that it will involve communicating with a much larger group of people. As well as anyone assigned directly to your project, you will typically need to communicate with:

- senior management;
- colleagues;
- customers;
- suppliers;
- family and friends.

While you may not normally think of these people as being part of your team, in a sense they are. First, because you cannot succeed without them. And second, because they all *want* the project to succeed: senior management because the project is important to the organization (otherwise, why would they have asked you to undertake it?), colleagues because the project almost certainly complements work they are doing, customers (whether internal or external to the organization) because they want the end result, suppliers because they want your business and family and friends simply because they want *you* to succeed.

This chapter contains some guidelines on communicating with each of these groups, and then describes how to create a simple colour-coded display to represent the lines of communication required within the project.

Senior managers

Organizations vary tremendously in the quality of communication between different levels of management. You may be fortunate enough to work in an organization in which you feel very comfortable asking managers for help or advice, and in which everyone views themselves as team players. In this case, you probably already view senior management as part of your team – people you can speak freely with about the problems and failures encountered along the way.

At the opposite extreme, you may work in a bureaucracy-bound organization in which hierarchy is everything and the degree of political intrigue makes Watergate look like a straightforward business transaction. In this latter case, the only advice I can offer is either get out, or learn to play politics. Such organizations are not geared to achieving results, and figuring out how to survive in them is an area in which I have little experience, and no desire to add to that experience.

Most organizations, conveniently, fall somewhere between the two. It is worth remembering, though, that even if your managers seem unapproachable, the fact that you have been given the project makes it a pretty safe bet that (a) the objective is one the organization wants you to achieve, and will therefore be willing to support you in achieving, and (b) your manager, and his or her managers, are confident in your ability to succeed, and will rely on you to do whatever it takes – including asking for help and additional resources as necessary.

Clarify your authority

The first step in relating to senior management is to determine precisely how much authority you have before you begin the project. Run through your timeline step by step to determine precisely what you can decide on your own, and what requires authorization from above. (You should, of course, use your commonsense in deciding the level of detail required, but beware of making assumptions which may turn out to be inaccurate.) This process may seem tedious, and your manager(s) may want to skate over it, but failure to clarify this point risks delay at best, as you wait for your next step to be approved, and catastrophe at worst, if senior management refuse you permission to implement a crucial part of your action plan.

Clarifying your authority is particularly important if you do not have authority over the budget. If you cannot raise cheques yourself, you need to ensure that the budget-controller understands who will need to be paid and when. Even multinational corporations have had conference centre bookings cancelled because the centre was promised payment on a specified date and the person needed to authorize the payment or sign the cheque was unavailable at the time.

In general, you want to aim for as much authority as possible, while at the same time ensuring that you have access to senior managers for advice and assistance as required.

In those areas where you have *not* been given authority, try to obtain approval for the whole action plan now, before you begin, rather than having to wait for authority later. Include your contingency plans in this process: explain what you plan to do in each contingency, and seek approval for these actions also – when disaster strikes, you will need to be able to act quickly.

If you cannot solicit advance approval, include waiting for authorization in your timeline. Ask the manager(s) concerned how long approval is likely to take, then double this when you add it to your timeline. Make sure managers know when decisions will be required. Ideally, give each manager concerned a written summary of the dates by which different decisions will be required. In practice, this may call for some diplomacy! Secretaries are good allies in this regard, and it is well worth taking the time to develop good relations with those of your managers. They may then be happy to make a note of the dates themselves, and give their bosses a gentle nudge at the appropriate time.

View senior managements as consultants. In theory at least, they have more experience than you, and are likely to have solved many of your problems themselves at some point. Do not be afraid to ask for advice – most people are flattered that you value their expertise – although, again, you will want to ensure that you are going about it in the right way: ensuring that it is a convenient time to ask, for example.

Your directly assigned team

A detailed discussion of personnel management techniques is clearly beyond the scope of this book! You know your team better than anyone else, and will know (or be learning) from experience the best way to relate to each member. All I will do here is add a few guidelines on managing your team in the context of managing a specific project.

First, if the team is being assigned to you specifically for this one project, try to pick your own team – especially if time is tight. While you will want to ensure that you have the appropriate collection of skills and expertise for the job, the ability to work together *as* a team is as vital as any technical skill, and it is almost always easier to work with a team you know. Your team members will, like anyone else, have weaknesses, but you will know these and be able to take them into account. If you know that James always delivers his assignment 24 hours late, or that Christine will need a five-minute pep-talk each morning, you can allow for this in your planning. Unknown weaknesses, however, cannot be managed until they become apparent.

Once you have completed the timeline, give everyone a copy – so that they can see how their own work fits into the overall project – but also prepare individual timelines for each team member. If you chose your project tracks as suggested in Chapter 2, with one person or department responsible for each track, this will simply be a case of reading off the actions along each track.

Begin with a team briefing on the whole project. This ensures that everyone is being given exactly the same information, and will begin to create a sense of a team. Let everyone know the objectives as well as the actions required, and invite suggestions on how the overall action plan can be improved – the team may be able to suggest things that others have missed, particularly if they are working in a specialist field, and studies have demonstrated that people work much more effectively on a project if they had a hand in its design.

Once the team briefing is complete, schedule time to brief each person on their own role. Do not be tempted to rush this process. Go through everything carefully, and allow plenty of time for questions. Ask each team member specifically if they have any doubts or concerns about the task: if so, you want to know about and overcome them now, not once you are in the middle of the project. This process will be as valuable in generating the type of open communication you want as in ensuring that you share a common understanding of the job to be done.

Just as you need to be sure of your own authority, make sure that you specify the authority held by each member of your team. Run through the same process you ran through with *your* managers, trying to make all the decisions made in advance and clarifying what will need to be approved and when during the project.

Make yourself available to your team. Offer your services as a consultant, trouble-shooter and sympathetic ear, and allow time for this in your schedule each day (scheduling your time is covered in the following chapter). Depending on your working style, you can achieve this with either an open-door policy, where any of your team can come to you at any time, or have a fixed period of about half an hour each day when you are specifically available to your team.

If your team will have to work evenings or weekends, when you may not be around, consider giving them your home phone number. While you may not like the idea of taking business calls at home, this can be a very effective way of demonstrating your commitment to supporting your team, and in practice it is often the knowledge that they *can* call you, rather than actually doing so, that makes the difference.

Cellphones and pagers can also be invaluable if you are likely to be away from your office at a time when your team may need to reach you. This topic is discussed in detail in Chapter 9.

Make the project timeline and project maps available to the whole team. If you do not want people to have free access to your office, you may want to mount these displays on a wall in an open-plan office area where everyone can see them. If your team members are scattered throughout the company, make copies of the timelines and maps, and encourage members to create their own project maps for their own areas of responsibility.

Delegate as much as possible without simply dumping the work on to somebody else. Your most important function is to maintain an overview of the project, to know how the project as a whole is progressing, and you cannot do this effectively if you allow yourself to become too involved in any one aspect of it.

Nobody can tell you when to delegate and when to do the job yourself – only you can judge what is appropriate given everyone's workload, expertise and so on – but take into account your strengths and weaknesses. For example, if you are a poor delegator, taking the view that it is quicker to do the job yourself rather than explain it to someone else, ask yourself whether this will be true the tenth time you find yourself performing a similar task. It may be worth investing a little extra time now in training people in order to allow yourself more free time later on.

Bear in mind, too, the effect that delegation – or its absence – will have on your team. There are dangers in both over- and under-delegation: over-delegate, and your team will resent the fact that you do not seem to be pulling your weight; under-delegate, and your team will begin to feel that you do not value or trust them. The key here is to encourage open communication, and to be willing to be flexible in order to keep your team happy.

Colleagues

Colleagues working on other projects within the organization may not play much practical part in the project, but at the very least can offer moral support, and they will often be able to make helpful suggestions.

Consulting colleagues may not always be practical, of course. Some projects are so commercially sensitive that information is released on a strict 'need to know' basis, and there may be other semi-sensitive projects where a newsletter would be too risky. Where a project does not need to be confidential, however, keep colleagues informed about the project. You might like to consider issuing a brief internal newsletter for other departments within the organization. This could be monthly, weekly or even daily, depending on the scale of the project. It is amazing how many times a naïve question from someone without specialist knowledge will prompt a simpler and cheaper solution to a problem.

Invite constructive suggestions, but make sure that you do not let a good idea sway you from the objectives of the project. The Managing Director of British Telecom's Business Communications Division keeps a list of his objectives on his desk; if somebody comes to him with a good idea, he checks it against his objectives before deciding whether or not to act on it. My own suggested personal management system, which is also very strongly objective-driven, is covered in Chapter 6.

The outside world

Customers and suppliers form a crucial part of your team. Your customer – be it an internal division of your own organization, or one or more external organizations – should be the guiding light behind the entire project. The very first test of our project objective in Chapter 1 was 'the customer test' (will the project genuinely benefit the customer?) and you can continue to invite customer input during the project itself. Virtually all software houses develop software in association with selected customers. These customers are given what is known as a beta-test version of the software, and invited to report faults, make suggestions and generally critique the product. The feedback from these customers is then used to develop the marketable version of the software. It may well be worth instigating your own 'beta-test' procedures to ensure that the product you bring to the market really is the product your customers want.

This is particularly important if the project is being undertaken for a single customer. In the case of a 'public' product, consumer opinion will vary; if one customer hates it, another may love it. When you have only one customer, however, the job specification is simple: provide what the client wants.

Suppliers are almost as important. If you rely on outside suppliers, you can only deliver what you have promised if your suppliers deliver what *they* have promised (except, of course, that you have contingency plans for dealing with isolated failures).

Fortunately, just as your customers call the shots with your project, you call the shots with your suppliers. In all but a few specialist areas, supply normally outstrips demand, and suppliers are only too well aware of this fact. If they do not perform, you can and will go elsewhere. I am not suggesting a confrontational approach to dealing with suppliers; quite the reverse. But it is worth remembering that a good supplier will do almost anything to help provided that the contract remains profitable. And if your supplier does not fit this description, look elsewhere.

In principle, a good supplier will aim to provide the best possible service to each of its customers, but a customer who makes an effort to establish a close working relationship with a supplier will invariably get the best service in difficult times. My wife used to run a desktop publishing company which relied on outside printing companies. She established friendly relations with two companies in particular, taking the time to chat with them, always letting them know if the client had decided not to proceed on a job for which they had quoted, and even sending 'thank you' notes to them when they had completed jobs. This paid dividends when she needed a rush job – they would squeeze in her work ahead of other jobs, and go to all lengths to ensure that it was delivered on time, simply because they liked doing business with her and knew that their efforts were appreciated.

It is particularly worth cultivating the junior staff of your suppliers. They are rarely appreciated or acknowledged, and remember well those who take the trouble to treat them with respect. And, despite their apparent lack of power, it is often junior staff who can make the difference in getting a job done faster than would otherwise be possible.

Family and friends

Your family and friends can play a vital role not just in the success of your project, but also in your sanity during it. Include them in the project, and let them know in advance of any heavy time commitments so that you can ensure that your family and social life does not get lost in the process. This subject is discussed in more detail in Chapter 8.

In general

Never be afraid to ask for help and advice. Most people love to be given the chance to demonstrate their expertise and spend time talking about one of their pet subjects, if only we would ask.

I was involved in a project recently to launch a subscription-based newsletter. I knew very little about the target market of the publication, and was looking for a consultant to advise me on the area. I phoned two casual acquaintances in the field to see if they could give me some initial pointers, and between them they told me everything I needed to know. One of them even called me back a few days later to tell me he had been giving the project some thought, and would I be interested in a few more ideas?

Drawing up your lines of communication

We often think of communication as random and unpredictable, rather than something which can be planned and managed. This is, of course, true to an extent. And yet, as we have seen, all action is ultimately a form of communication, and we fully expect to be able to plan and manage actions.

The key to planning and managing communication is, as with any other project, to be clear about your objectives for the communication. The simplest way to achieve this clarity is using a visual display of your lines of communication.

Take a piece of A4 paper. Write 'Me' in a circle in the centre of the sheet. Now think about each of the above categories of your 'extended' team. For each category, use a different shape. For example:

- senior management = rectangle;
- your directly-assigned team = circle;
- colleagues = parallelogram;
- customers = triangle;
- suppliers = octagon;
- family and friends = clouds.

Now, write the names of each of your contacts inside the appropriately-shaped box, for example you might have a supplier called Acme Trading. Repeat this process for each member of your extended team.

Now, connect the boxes by drawing lines with coloured pens. The colour of the line represents the type of communication. For example:

- authority/approval = red;
- information = green;
- instructions/orders/requests = dark blue;

- delivered work/supplies = light blue;
- invitations = purple;
- acceptances = pink.

Place one or more arrows on the lines to indicate the direction of communication. For example, if you provide information to a senior manager who will then provide approval to you, you would have a green line from you to the manager, and a red line returning from the manager to you as in Figure 5.1.

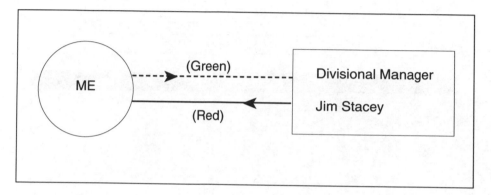

Figure 5.1 Creating a lines of communications map

Complete the entire diagram for an instant visual summary of your main lines of communication. You can, of course, add to the diagram at a later date.

Managing your communication

Use a form as shown in Figure 5.2 to plan your main communications. These forms can be used for meetings, one-to-one conversations, telephone calls and videoconferences.

Before each communication, summarize your objective(s) together with your planned agenda/structure for the communication. The Action Points section will be used during the communication to record whatever action is agreed – the top section to list actions to be completed by you, and the bottom section to record actions to be completed by the other person.

Again, apply your own judgement as to when to use the forms. It would clearly be silly to use them for casual and routine communication, but they can be an enormous help in ensuring that important meetings, telephone calls and so on actually achieve what is required of them. They are particularly useful when time is short and you want to ensure that everything is covered without wasting time. Simply use a highlighter pen to cross through each objective and agenda item as it is completed: the highlighter clearly marks the item as done, but still allows you to read what was written.

COMMUNICATION PLANNER

| | | | | | Date | | Time | |

| Who | | What | |

OBJECTIVES

| AGENDA / PLAN | ACTIONS AGREED |

Figure 5.2 A blank communication planner form

SUMMARY

- We have grown up with the myth of the lone hero; this myth is a dangerous one for project managers. Most projects are the work of winning teams.

- Virtually any action step in a timeline can be viewed as a form of communication. Defining your lines of communication is thus key to the success of the project.

- Your 'extended team' can be defined as all those with whom you will need to communicate to achieve the project objective. This will typically include senior management, colleagues, customers, suppliers and even family and friends.

- It is important to clarify with senior management where your authority begins and ends. Where an action will require approval, seek this approval ahead of time, including approval which would become necessary under one of your contingency plans.

- If you can, pick your own team – you are then dealing with known quantities, and can allow for known weaknesses.

- Give everyone a copy of the master timeline, together with an individual timeline for their own accountabilities.

- Brief the team as a team on the whole project, then brief each member individually on their own role. Specify the authority given to each team member.

- Make yourself available to your team. If an open-door policy does not work for you, set aside a specific time each day to be available to your team for help and advice.

- Avoid over- or under-delegating. Encourage open communication, so that you will know if you have got the balance wrong.

- Consult colleagues if security requirements allow, but do not let a 'good idea' sway you from your objectives.

- If possible, instigate a 'Beta-test' procedure to enable you to benefit from customer feedback during the development stage.

- Make friends with your suppliers, especially junior staff. This will reap dividends if you ever need a special favour.

- Do not let your family and social life disappear amidst a heavy workload.

- Never be afraid to ask for help and advice – most people love to talk about their pet subjects and show off their expertise.

- Draw up a visual summary of your main lines of communication as described towards the end of the chapter, and use communications planners to ensure that your meetings and phone calls achieve their objectives.

6

TURNING THE ACTION PLAN INTO ACTION

or There is no such thing as time management

Regaining control of your schedule is a little like regaining control of a skidding car: you have to resist your instinctive reaction and respond intelligently instead. In a skidding car, that instinctive reaction is to slam on the brakes; in a tight schedule, the instinctive reaction is to try to find more time. Both reactions have the effect of leaving you even further out of control.

Most of us do not control our schedules; our schedules control us. This chapter – together with Chapter 7 on taking control of your paperwork – provide the tools you need to bring your schedule under control, and keep it that way.

More time is not the answer

> Even if you're on the right track, you'll get run over if you just sit there.
>
> Will Rogers

Whenever we find ourselves facing a seemingly impossible workload, our instinctive response is to wish we had more time. This wish is futile in two senses. First, we cannot have more time. Whether we are a new-born baby or the chairperson of a multinational corporation, we all receive exactly the same amount of time: 60 seconds per minute, 60 minutes per hour, 24 hours per day. Extra seconds, minutes or hours do not materialize because we have a busy schedule. We cannot put time aside in a slack period to use during a busy one. We cannot borrow time now and promise to repay it later. We cannot apply for a 'time-rise' because we really deserve one.

Second, even if we *could* obtain more time, it would not help. We would just take on more work, and soon we would be back in exactly the same position as before.

That is why I do not refer to time management. There is no such thing. What we *can* manage is the way we use our time, that is *action management*. And that is what this chapter is all about: ensuring that we manage our actions so as to meet our objectives.

The difference is not just a matter of semantics. It is an attitude of mind. Call something 'time management' and you instinctively think that the answer has something to do with time. It does not – whether you have two hours a day or twelve hours a day available to you; what matters is whether you dedicate those hours to the actions that will have the greatest impact in bringing you closer to your objectives. Calling it 'action management' puts the emphasis where it belongs: examining and adjusting your actions, not your working hours.

If you want to see that it really isn't about time, try the following experiment. Take something you have to do that you think will take about 20 minutes. Now do it in 10 minutes. Do it now, before you read any further.

Do not draw too many conclusions from this experiment just yet. I am not suggesting that you can do this ad infinitum, otherwise all your tasks could eventually be accomplished in an infinitely small amount of time! But it does indicate that perhaps the amount of time is less important than the way in which we use that time.

The schedule paradox

If you've got time to reorganize your schedule, you do not need to. If you cannot possibly spare the time to do so, you cannot afford not to.

Resolving this paradox requires boldness. Investing time in reorganizing the way you manage your actions will take time – no 'ifs', no 'buts'. But I guarantee that you will recoup the time invested in this chapter within two weeks, maximum. This means that in two weeks, you will be even. In two weeks and one day, you will be ahead. And you will be ahead from that day on.

This does, of course, require commonsense. If you are in the final two weeks of an urgent project, this is not the time to start reorganizing yourself. But if you find yourself *always* in the final two weeks of an urgent project, with no time to spare, organizing yourself is the most urgent item on your list.

This system requires the following time investment:

- approximately half a day to a day at the end of each year;
- approximately 30 minutes at the end of each month;
- approximately 30 minutes at the end of each week;
- approximately 10 minutes at the end of each day.

You can expect to spend about 50 per cent longer than this during the first week or two, while you familiarize yourself with the system.

As we will see in a moment, though, the system is designed to increase your effectiveness from a typical 20–50 per cent to 80 per cent plus. This means that, if you work a 40-hour week, you will save between 12 and 24 hours *per week*. That is between 48 and 96 hours per month. Or 576 to 1152 hours per year – equivalent to 72 to 144 full 8-hour working days! If you work more than 40 hours a week, the time savings will be proportionately greater. (After reading Chapter 8, you will begin to build up an idea of just how much greater.) All in all, it is a fine return on your investment.

The principle behind action management

The principle behind effective action management is an absurdly simple one: ensuring that your actions – that is, the things you spend your time doing – are those most likely to produce the results you want.

It sounds too simple to be worth discussing until you take a look at a typical day's schedule: how many things that you carried out today were totally aligned to your objectives for the year, month and week? And how many were just nuisances to be handled? If you are honest, you will probably find that less than 50 per cent of your day is spent performing actions which are designed to forward your project. And the figure could be as low as 20 per cent. Another way of looking at this would be to say that your effectiveness as a project manager probably lies in the range 20–50 per cent.

The action management system presented in this chapter, together with the paper-handling systems detailed in Chapter 7, are designed to increase your effectiveness to 80 per cent or more. In other words, 80 per cent or more of your time will be spent on work that is directly geared to meeting your personal and professional objectives.

Action management begins with objectives

As always, effective management begins with clarifying your objectives. You already have a clear objective for your project, and your timeline provides regular sub-objectives – milestones – along the way. Taking the principle one step further, you could view your daily actions as yet further sub-objectives to be achieved each day.

For your specific project, you can simply transfer your project objectives and action steps across to the action management system described here (of which more later). But the action management system described has a wider application than just a single project: you can use it to set and co-ordinate *all* your objectives for a period of a year or more, and then ensure that your schedule is calculated to fulfil these objectives.

The system is based on a series of forms. Buying this book entitles you to make as many photocopies of these forms as you like *for your own personal use*; it does not entitle you to copy them for other people – you would have to buy additional copies of the book if you would like colleagues to use the system also. When copying the forms, I recommend that you use a photocopier with an enlargement facility to copy them onto A4 paper.

The following text talks you through the process of using the system in its fullest sense: to plan *all* your objectives for a year or more. If you intend to use it for a single project only, you should still read the text below to understand the principles of the system, but completing the sheets will be much quicker as you are essentially only transferring information from the timeline to the sheets below. Always keep the objective → actions principle in mind: for each day's work, you should know what you are trying to achieve (the objective) and how you intend to achieve it (the actions).

The year planner

Every year, millions of people make New Years' resolutions. Most of these resolutions last a matter of weeks at best. These abandoned resolutions do not only include personal objectives like giving up smoking or beginning an exercise programme, they also include business objectives which are written down with honourable intentions at the beginning of the calendar or financial year and then quickly forgotten as the routine work piles up.

The reason these personal and professional objectives are so often abandoned is simply that they exist in isolation: they are not integrated into our daily lives. We have our great dreams and visions on the one hand, and our everyday schedule on the other. And since our everyday schedule determines how we spend our time, it is the everyday activities that are achieved rather than our dreams and visions.

The action management system described here overcomes this difficulty by integrating the two, so that our everyday schedule is based on, and is designed to achieve, the objectives we set at the beginning of the year.

I said earlier that the system requires an investment of half a day to a day at the end of each year. This time does not have to be at the end of a calendar or financial year – you can begin it any time you like, but it is preferable to set objectives for a full 12-month period or more.

This initial stage will require a certain amount of quiet, uninterrupted thought. I suggest a bank holiday or weekend somewhere where you will not be disturbed. Take a plentiful supply of paper. I often find that a large (A3) sketchpad and some coloured pens and pencils help me think – I literally sketch out ideas. Take 10–20 copies of the year planner form (Figure 6.1) – you will almost certainly work through several draft year plans before you finally produce one you want to keep.

Start by reviewing the year just ending. Look at what you hoped to achieve during the year, and what you actually did achieve. Identify your most important successes – those which please you the most – and the most disappointing failures – what you would loved to have achieved but did not. Include both personal and professional matters.

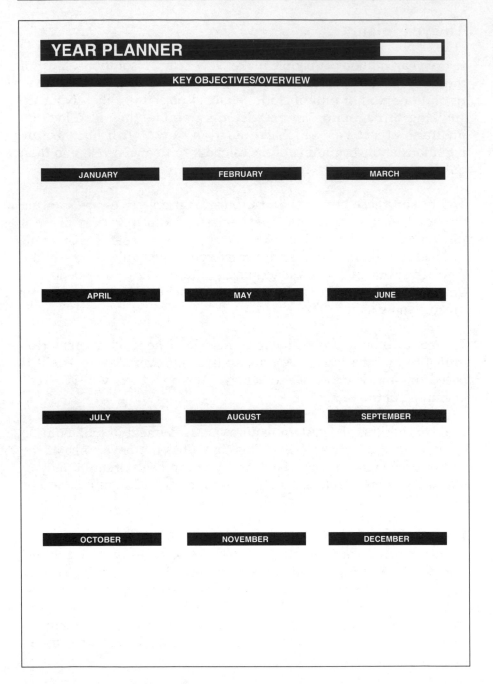

Figure 6.1 Year planner

Next, take a blank sheet of paper and write down anything that comes to mind that you would like to achieve in the forthcoming 12 months. Do not censor anything because it seems silly or unrealistic – you may not achieve everything you write down, or include everything in your year plan, but you do not want to omit something important just because you cannot yet see how achievement is possible. Give yourself a generous amount of time for this stage, at least an hour, but take as much time as you feel you need.

Now choose the goals that most appeal to you. I recommend that you restrict this to between three and five major goals for the year. Remember, you are looking at goals that will take several months to a year to achieve; leave aside any short-term ones for the moment. You want to find a balance between 'pie in the sky' goals which you are not prepared to act on, and mundane goals which you would probably succeed in anyway. There is no point in setting objectives unless you are prepared to work for them; equally, there is no point in writing down things that generally happen of their own accord.

Take time to word them carefully: think about *exactly* what it is you want to achieve. Remember, everything else – your monthly, weekly and daily objectives and actions – will be based on the objectives as you state them here. Run them through the tests given in Chapter 1, except that in this case *you* are the customer!

Once you have your objectives for the year, write them in the top section of the form (Figure 6.1). Give each one a colour code – either use a different coloured pen for each, or put a coloured sticker beside each one.

You are now ready to set your primary monthly objectives. Take each annual objective in turn, and ask yourself what would have to be undertaken each month in order to achieve the objective. This is like a simplified form of timelining. If the objective is complex, you may even find it useful to use the timelining system described in Chapter 2.

Write in these monthly objectives under the appropriate month. For example, if one of your annual objectives is to increase your company's market share by 25 per cent, you might begin in January by ordering an analysis of the current market – what is the total market for the product or service, and who currently holds what percentage of that market? In February you might commission consumer research to find out what factors influence choice of supplier, and how you currently rate against these factors. In the period March–May you might put into place the necessary changes, in June create a marketing plan to bring the changes to the attention of consumers, test the campaign in July and launch the full-scale marketing effort from August onwards.

Again, use the colour coding to tie the monthly objectives to the annual ones. So if your annual objective to increase your market share by 25 per cent is coded red, all of the above monthly objectives would be coloured red also.

MONTH PLANNER	
OVERVIEW	**KEY GOALS**
01	
02	
03	
04	
05	
06	
07	
08	
09	
10	
11	
12	
13	
14	
15	
16	
17	
18	
19	
20	
21	
22	
23	
24	
25	
26	
27	
28	
29	
30	
31	

Figure 6.2 Month planner

Once you have completed your year plan, by setting monthly objectives to fulfil each of your annual ones, you are ready to create more detailed monthly plans.

The month planner

The month planners are where you begin turning your general objectives into specific plans. For each month, take the monthly objectives from the year planner and transfer them to each of your twelve month planners, but go into greater detail. Turn each objective into several sub-objectives. There is no fixed way of doing this, just divide them up in a way that makes sense to you, but aim to arrive at sub-objectives that will take a week or less to achieve (Figure 6.2).

You may be able to complete month planners for the whole year now, or you may want to fill in only the overall objectives for the month, and then complete them in detail at the end of each preceding month. Use whichever approach makes the most sense to you.

Whether you complete your month planners all at the same time, or on a month-by-month basis, the next stage is the same: look at when you will tackle each of the monthly objectives. Use the overview column to map out a rough schedule for this work. You should also mark in any previously scheduled work and/or meetings, but only items that occupy half a day or more. The idea of this sheet is simply to give you a general picture of your month, not every detail.

Continue this process until you have a general schedule for each of your monthly objectives.

The week planner

The week planner is where your translate your general schedule into specifics. You begin by setting your weekly objectives for each week in the month. You already have week-sized objectives on your month planner, so this is simply a case of assigning each one to a specific week. You might also like to add in an objective that captures the spirit of the kind of week you want to have – you might, for example, include an objective along the lines of 'deal with each unwanted interruption in five minutes or less'. See Figure 6.3.

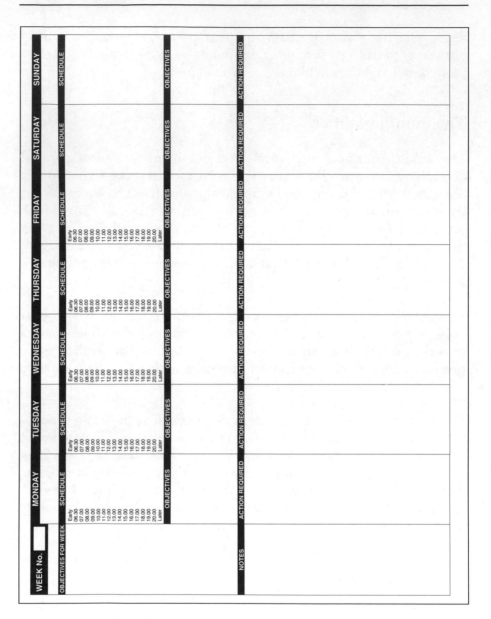

Figure 6.3 Week planner

The next stage is to turn the weekly objectives into daily objectives. Again, you may like to do this a month at a time, or you may prefer to do it a week at a time, at the end of the preceding week. Either way, you are simply dividing each of your weekly objectives into chunks that can be completed in a single day.

Finally, you will look at the daily actions required to fulfil these daily objectives. I suggest you do this one week at a time, at the end of the preceding week. If you work a normal eight-hour day with a one-hour lunchbreak, do not schedule more than five hours' worth of actions per day for reasons discussed below.

The day planner

The day planner is simply a more detailed version of the information from the week planner and is shown in Figure 6.4. Simply transfer each day's details onto a day planner sheet, expanding the detail as required. The idea of this sheet is that you have a single sheet of paper to work from that contains your work for that one day and nothing else. It thus encourages you to concentrate on the work in hand, without being distracted by anything required later in the week.

As you complete each action, cross it through with a highlighter pen. This marks it as complete much more clearly than a simple tick or line, but still enables you to read the text so that you can refer back to it later in the day should the need arise.

At the end of the day, reschedule any actions you did not complete by transferring them onto the appropriate week planner. If you notice you are consistently failing to complete the items on your day planner, you are clearly scheduling too much work and need to adjust your schedule accordingly. Try creating a schedule that is slightly less than you know you can achieve; that way, you end the day with a 'win' – you complete everything – and can even start to get ahead of your schedule. If you consistently schedule too much work, on the other hand, you will feel that you are constantly running just to keep up.

I said above that you should not schedule more than five hours' work in an eight-hour day. The reason for this is that, aside from your one-hour lunchbreak (which you should not skip – see Chapter 8), you will typically spend two hours a day dealing with routine work and unexpected distractions. You will be able to reduce this two-hour period as you begin implementing this system and take the measures recommended in Chapter 7, but you can never eliminate the routine and the unexpected, so include it in your time allowances.

When you do find yourself doing work that is not on your day planner, stop! Ask yourself whether the item really needs to be done at all (could it be delegated or even ignored?) and, if so, whether it needs to be done today (could it be postponed?). If it *does* need to be done today, add it to your day planner. There are two reasons for this. First, when you come to the end of the day you have an accurate record of what you achieved. All too often we find ourselves doing unexpected work, and then wonder why our action

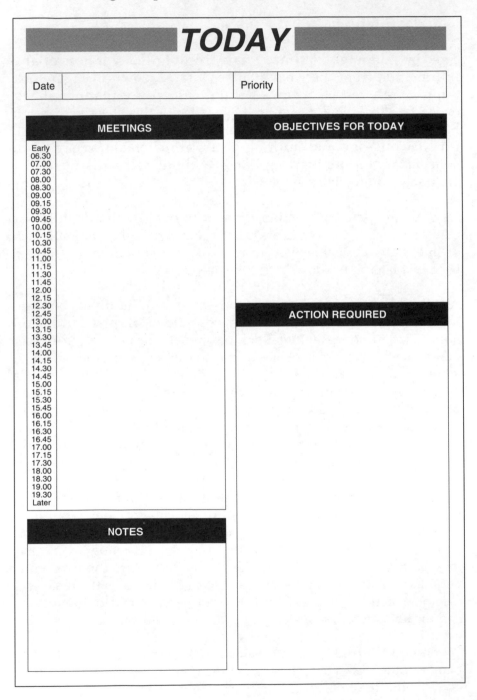

Figure 6.4 Day planner

list remains incomplete at the end of the day. Second, you will begin to develop a sense of the nature, frequency and duration of your most common distractions, and plan your schedule accordingly.

Prioritizing actions

There are numerous systems for prioritizing actions. Some are manual techniques, others use computer software. If you find them helpful, by all means use them, but if you want a fast, simple and to-the-point method of prioritizing your daily actions, try this one.

Forget about putting your actions into order of priority. Just look at your action list and ask yourself which single item is the most important right now? (Bear in mind that your answer will depend on *when* you ask the question – an action which is low priority now could be top priority in a week's time.) That is all you need to know. It does not matter in what order the rest should be: you know what most needs doing, so do that. When you have done that, ask the same question again. That is all there is to it!

Be particularly careful to apply this test to interruptions! If somebody appears in your office, a piece of paper arrives on your desk or the phone rings, give yourself 30 seconds to think. If it is a visitor or a phone call, ask them to hold on while you finish something, then ask yourself whether the distraction is your highest priority right now. If not, find a way to postpone it – arrange another time to speak or meet, let the piece of paper lie in your in-tray (the following chapter should enable you to cut your incoming paperwork by up to 80 per cent) or whatever it takes. And if you *do* decide to make the interruption your priority action, put it on your action list so that you will know where the time went when you review your day.

Important *versus* urgent

Important and urgent are two entirely separate concepts. An action is important if failure to complete it would have serious consequences; it is urgent if there is a limited time in which it is *possible* to complete it. Sometimes the two coincide, and an action is both important and urgent, but it is equally possible to confuse the two.

Your aim should be to concentrate on important actions. Too often, the important is neglected in favour of 'urgent' trivia. Just because the opportunity to do something is about to expire it does not mean that you have to do it; in many cases, the consequences of delaying an important action are far more serious than those of completely failing to complete a less important but more urgent action. Yet we do not see that at the time because we feel pressured by the urgency.

Train yourself to be suspicious of all urgent actions. First, is the deadline as real as it appears? It is very often possible to extend a deadline on an action just by making a brief phone call. Second, what would happen if you totally ignored the action? If the consequences would be trivial, perhaps you do not need to do it at all.

'Quick and dirty' approaches

Where an urgent action *does* need to be handled, ask yourself whether there is a 'quick and dirty' way of handling it. 'Quick and dirty' approaches are ones that do not meet your usual standards, but carry out the job as well as it actually needs to be done. This is a vital distinction for those of us with perfectionist tendencies. We all too often spend an hour doing something perfectly, when we could have spent ten minutes doing an imperfect job that was, none the less, perfectly adequate for the purpose.

Clearly work that will be seen by clients should be of a high standard. And if – like me – you enjoy excellence for its own sake, it may well pay dividends to do a proper job on internal projects also. But always ask yourself whether you are doing a better job than is justified. If doing a perfect job on something relatively unimportant means that you are later forced to do a less-than-perfect job on something more important, your perfectionism is working against you.

Turning the world into an action management system

The point of writing things down is so that you do not have to clutter up your mind with lots of detail: to enable you to give your full attention to the matter in hand. But writing things down is only one way of creating an action management system: you can also use physical objects, technological aids and even people as part of your action management system.

Take a simple example. I have a meeting to go to in an hour's time. Before I leave, I need to retrieve a few bits of paper from a sling file and take them with me. I could write this down as an action, but then I would have to be sure that I would check that particular action before I left the office. Instead, I take a far simpler and ultimately more reliable approach: I take the file out of my filing cabinet and put it in my doorway! That way I will see it when I leave and will remember to retrieve the papers I need. Sounds silly? Perhaps, but it works. And that is what I am interested in – systems which are simple, quick and effective.

You can use this principle in a whole host of ways. Do you forget to check your answerphone when you come in? Move the answerphone so that it is the first thing you see when you come in through the door. Need to make a personal call next time you take a coffee break? Stick a note on your coffee cup. Need to pick up some papers from home? Phone your answerphone at home and leave yourself a message.

Technology can also be used to prompt you. You can buy pocket organizers, which will prompt you with a text message at a pre-programmed time, from about £20. If you use an electronic mail service, it may have the facility to deliver messages on a specific date – you can send messages to yourself to be sure that the item receives your attention. If you have a direct-line phone on a digital exchange, you can programme a 'reminder call' for just a few pence – a ringing phone has less chance of being ignored than a watch alarm or similar.

You can also use people as part of your action management system. This is a large part of the job of a secretary, of course, but if you do not have a secretary you can use other peoples': if you need to speak to somebody on a certain date, for example, you can ring their secretary and ask if she would arrange for them to call you on that date.

Make a note of the type of things you typically forget, then look at how you could use the outside world as part of your action management system.

The acid test

I will make no excuse for repeating this advice at regular intervals throughout the book: do what works for you. If a system works for you, it does not matter how odd it might be (like my habit of leaving files in my doorway) – use it! Conversely, if something does not work for you, it does not matter how carefully designed or pretty it may be – do not waste your time on it.

All the recommendations and suggestions in this chapter are just that. For example, I recommend scheduling slightly less than you know you can handle, so that you end the day with a 'win,' completing everything on your schedule. This works for me. Some people, however, prefer the pressure of an overcrowded schedule, as this keeps them on their toes and helps them avoid distractions. Find out what works best for you, then stick to that.

SUMMARY

- Most of us do not control our schedules; our schedules control us.

- More time is not the answer to a busy schedule; even if it were possible, we would soon fill this additional time with extra work.

- What is needed is not time management, but *action management*.

- If you can spare the time to reorganize yourself, you do not need to; if you cannot possibly find the time, you cannot afford not to reorganize yourself.

- The system outlined in this chapter requires an investment of time, but will gain you more time than it takes within two weeks.

- Most of us operate at 20–50 per cent effectiveness; that is, 20–50 per cent of our time is spent forwarding our projects. The approach described in this chapter will enable you to increase this to 80 per cent plus.

- The principle behind effective action management is absurdly simple: ensure that the bulk of your time is spent on actions which will produce the results you want. Most people do not do this.

- Effective action management begins with objectives, then divides those objectives into smaller and smaller chunks until you have a list of daily actions which are forwarding your annual objectives. The forms contained in this chapter are designed to ensure that your everyday schedule is geared to your goals for the year.

- Prioritizing actions is simple: look at your list and ask yourself which action is the most important right now: do that action. The priority of the remaining actions is academic. Repeat this process each time you complete an action.

- Apply this priority test to all interruptions. Interruptions are often given a higher priority than they merit.

- Distinguish the important from the urgent. If something is urgent but not important, ask yourself (a) if the deadline is as real as it appears, and (b) whether the action needs to be completed at all.

- If you have perfectionist tendencies, do not let your perfectionism work against you. Use 'quick and dirty' approaches to unimportant actions to enable you to perform excellent work when it really counts.

- Use your environment as part of your action management system. Leave important files where you will see them, use technology such as organizers with alarms, arrange for other people to call you and so on.

- Do what works for you – no matter how eccentric it may appear to be.

7

OUTWITTING THE PAPERWORK

or A working environment that works

Paper is not an inanimate substance. It breeds, relentlessly, increasing its population year after year, unaffected by the emergence of the supposedly paperless office. In the UK, the amount of paper consumed is increasing at ten times the rate of population growth. Last year, we used the equivalent of more than 30 trillion sheets of A4 paper world-wide! Laid end to end, that is enough sheets to reach to the sun and back 30 times.

Used effectively and sparingly, paper can be a powerful aid to producing results. Used unthinkingly, paper can suffocate ideas, stifle productivity and drown projects. If you are serious about getting results, a clear, organized working environment is not a luxury, it is vital.

A clear working environment

> The reasonable man adapts himself to the conditions that surround him ... the unreasonable man adapts the surrounding conditions to himself ... thus all progress depends on the unreasonable man.
>
> George Bernard Shaw

A clear working environment is one in which you have instant access to all the information you need, with no excess clutter. It is an environment in which your paperwork serves you, not the other way round. It is an environment in which you not only *are* in control of the project, but you *feel* that you are in control of your project.

The reason most people do not organize their working environment properly is that they think they do not have time. In fact, nothing could be further from the truth. As with reorganizing your schedule, if you are busy, you do not have time not to organize your working environment.

Try a little test. Pick an item at random from your budget that you will buy-in from an outside supplier. Now find the supplier's fax number and the name of your contact at the company. How long did it take? Now pick another item, look up the cost on the budget and find the quote, estimate or other source of that costing. How long? Think of a letter or memo you sent to someone about three months ago. Find it. How long?

Try this test with half a dozen other items, chosen at random, and time how long it takes to find the information you need. If any item takes longer than 30 seconds, there is room for improvement; if anything takes longer than a minute, you urgently need an improved filing system.

Another test. If you were away from your desk and somebody placed a piece of paper on it, would it be immediately visible to you? Or would it be just one more sheet among the rest?

Try this one. Can you state with certainty that your in-tray does not contain something that should have been done yesterday? And that the percentage of irrelevant material in your tray is not in excess of 10 per cent?

How about this? You ask one of your team to prepare some information for you. Does it arrive in the exact form you require, or do you have to hunt through the report for the details you need?

Or this. If you were urgently called away from the office tonight, could you phone a colleague and tell them where to find out the precise status of the project, and where they could find any piece of information they might need?

If you passed all these tests, and your working environment also feels like a great place to work, you have no need of this chapter. Otherwise, read on.

Take charge of your in-tray!

The first stage in outwitting paperwork is to take charge of your in-tray: the source of, or inlet for, all paperwork. To do this you need to remove every piece of paper that does not belong there, and to sort what is left according to priority. This is a far easier process than you might think, provided you are willing to be sufficiently ruthless.

Most people have a fear of throwing away paper on the basis that they 'might need it some day'. This is true: you might. But unless there is a reasonable prospect of your requiring it in the foreseeable future, the total time you waste dealing with this category of information will far exceed the time it will take you to track down the same piece of information if and when you ever do need it.

So, here is a straightforward way to cut your in-tray down to size. It is unlikely to take more than 20 minutes, and will typically rid your in-tray of about 80 per cent of its content – a good investment of time by anybody's standards!

1 Take five plastic coloured wallets, and label them as follows:
   Red: Essential
   Yellow: On-track
   Green: Wants
   Blue: Some day
   Black: Reject
   (These are only suggested colours – change them if you wish.)

2 Put your project objective in front of you.

3 Now, check each piece of paper in your in-tray against your objective. Place each piece of paper into one of the five wallets:

   • *Essential*, if you cannot achieve the project objective without dealing with this piece of paper;
   • *On-track*, if the piece of paper relates directly to, and will forward, the project objective;
   • *Wants*, if the piece of paper relates to something you actively want to achieve, even if it does not relate to the project objective;
   • *Some day*, if the piece of paper has to be dealt with sometime, but does not actually bring you any closer to your objectives. This will describe all those non-urgent boring tasks that you know you cannot avoid indefinitely but, in all honesty, you will not deal with them a moment before you really have to;
   • *Reject*, if the piece of paper does not belong in any of the four other piles.

If you are typical, you will find that the Essential wallet is extremely thin, the On-track and Wants wallets thicker, the Some day pile is bulging a little and the Reject wallet is bursting at the seams!

Place all but the Reject wallet into your in-tray (the items still need to be dealt with, but are now prioritized). Now comes the ruthless part. The paper in your Reject wallet does not belong in your in-tray. If it is neither essential nor on-track for your project objectives, it is not something you want to do and neither is it one of life's unavoidable chores, it does not require your attention. Go through this wallet and do one of three things with each item:

- pass it on to somebody else;
- file it for future reference; or
- throw it away.

Now place the empty Reject wallet at the bottom of your in-tray.

Maintaining an effective in-tray

Whenever a fresh piece of paper arrives on your desk, immediately sort it into one of your five wallets. If it belongs in the Reject wallet, and is not worth filing, send it back to wherever it came from and ask that you be deleted from the distribution list. You are probably on hundreds of mailing lists for products you do not want, are circulated with memos that do not concern you and receive publications and reports that are of no relevance or interest to you. You can, of course, simply consign these to the bin, but if you want to rid yourself of them permanently, take a minute to send them back.

You can make the Reject process swift by printing some computer labels with instructions such as 'Return to sender – unwanted mail – Please delete me from your mailing list' for junk mail, and 'Your courtesy in circulating this is appreciated, but please delete me from the circulation list – Thank you' for memos, and so on. Then all you need do is slap on the appropriate sticky label and place the item in your out-tray.

Taking charge of your desk!

Next item on the agenda is to make sure that your desk is a working environment that works.

You might like to start by making sure that your office furniture is comfortable. Is your desk the right size and shape? Is your furniture attractive to look at, making you feel pleased to be working there each day? If not, consider changing it. While office furniture seems expensive, good quality furniture should last for many years, so the true cost is much lower than you might think. Let us say you spend £2000 on a good-quality desk, chair and filing system. At first glance it seems like a lot of money. But this level of quality should easily last ten years. A £2000 cost spread over ten years works out to less than £20 per month, or about £4 per week.

Someone earning £20000 a year, working 48 weeks a year, 35 hours a week, would have to gain three to four hours' additional productivity per week to justify this cost. Someone on £50000 a year would have to gain less than two hours. Would you gain this productivity if you had a working environment that really inspired you? If so, it is money well spent.

Whether or not you can afford or justify new furniture, is your desk arranged in the optimal layout? Do you have the items to hand that you use most often? Is your telephone within easy reach? If you use a personal computer a great deal, is it positioned exactly where you want it? If you use a computer only occasionally, is it on a side table, out of the way? Do you use a business card file frequently? If so, is it readily to hand? If you like natural light, are you near a window?

These questions are simply examples. Take a little time to observe yourself at work. Notice the conditions or items that you need most often, and check whether your office layout, desk arrangement, drawer contents and so on match your working patterns.

Always clear your desk at the end of each day. This not only means that you face a clean desk in the morning – generally more inspiring that one still covered in yesterday's work – but also means that you have to check through everything before you leave, ensuring that nothing gets overlooked.

Design a filing system to support you

Most people do not design their filing systems – they inherit them. Inherited systems are generally little more than repositories for information someone thought they might need someday. They are both inefficient, making it a chore to find the precise piece of paper you need, and a waste of space, containing masses of paperwork you do not need. What you need is an active filing system, containing only the information you actually need to refer to, and designed to enable you to find that information as quickly and easily as possible.

Start with a spring-clean of your files – go through each one, and throw away anything you no longer need. If you have archive files you cannot throw away but no longer use, put them in bank boxes and file them somewhere out of the way – they do not need to clutter up your active filing system. This process will probably reduce the information contained in your filing system by about 50 per cent.

Now that you have some space to work with, you can design an active filing system for your project. First, allocate one specific area for project files and nothing else. Depending on the size of the project, this might be a single drawer in a filing cabinet, or one or more entire filing cabinets.

Next, acquire some coloured sling files. Use the same colour coding as your project tracks (or as close as you can get). For example, if the Design track is coloured red, use red sling files for all paperwork concerned with design.

Run through each track on your timeline, and ask yourself what information you will need at each stage of the project. Design your filing system to match this. This might mean dividing up your files in quite a different way to conventional filing procedures. In some cases, you will need the same information at two or more points in the project; if so, consider photostatting the relevant papers and placing copies in all the relevant sling files. Although this might seem to contradict the principle of keeping paperwork to a minimum, it actually reduces the time and effort consumed by looking after your paperwork, which is what we are really trying to achieve.

Think about whether conventional sling files are the best means of filing all your information. If you have information you need to refer to on a daily basis, you might be better off filing it in a ring-binder which sits beside your desk. Again, follow the same colour coding with ring-binders, file tags and so on. If you have a ring-binder which contains information from more than one track, use coloured dividing sheets to indicate the different tracks – or even coloured paper.

It may be worth storing information electronically. The beginning of a project is not the time to begin setting up a database from scratch, but if you already use one, look at whether that might be an efficient way to store some of the information you need.

As with action management, the most important point about your filing system is that it works the way *you* want it to. It does not matter if the system you choose is a completely idiosyncratic one *as long as you can teach other people to use it if they need access.*

If the information you need changes rapidly, you may find it worthwhile to set up an indexed filing system. Briefly, you label your sling files with numbers rather than names, and keep a separate index of the current contents next to the filing cabinet. For example, you might label your Design files DES001, DES002 and so on. Then you produce an index which says 'DES001: Current design specifications,' 'DES002: Components list' and so on. Whenever you need to discard old information and replace it with new, you simply update the index.

Managing incoming information

The one problem with any paperwork management system is that paper arrives in the form decided by the person who sent it, not the form in which you require it. But while you cannot control the content or structure of much of the information you receive, you *can* control the information given to you by members of your team.

Much of the information being sent to you by your team members takes the form of regular progress reports. If you find that these contain too much information, too little information or are simply structured in an inconvenient way, consider designing forms for your team to use. A form allows you to control the nature, sequence and amount of information you receive. A sample form might look like the one shown in Figure 7.1.

Designing forms takes time, of course, but then so does wading through reams of unwanted information, or chasing up information you need but have not received.

Use your project maps

Project maps are effective only if you keep them updated. Ideally,

PROGRESS REPORT

Week ending [   ]   Report from [   ]

DUE FOR COMPLETION THIS WEEK	STATUS

CURRENT PROBLEMS / ALERTS

ANTICIPATED PROBLEMS / ALERTS

Figure 7.1 A sample weekly report form

you want to update them the moment something is progressed, but at worst they should be updated at the end of each day. If they do not seem to be moving, find out why not: is it because the project is stalled, or because your maps do not measure the work that is currently being done? If the former, you need to refer back to your timeline to identify the reason; if the latter, create an additional project map that *does* measure your current progress.

Complete actions 100 per cent

Some people habitually work on an action until 90 per cent complete, then become stuck or distracted and move on to something else. They then end up with a network of almost-finished actions littered around them.

This working pattern is fatal in project management. A project is one or more sequences of actions; a single incomplete action, if it lies on the critical path, or is allowed to become critical, can delay the whole project.

Even if an incomplete action does not delay the project, it cannot be marked as complete on your project map. Partially completing a whole series of actions will make it appear as if nothing much is happening, and momentum will be lost.

Incomplete actions also remain a background 'niggle'. Part of your attention will be distracted by the knowledge that you have left something undone, and you miss the tremendous satisfaction there is in knowing that a stage of the project is totally complete.

Clearly, there will be times when it is impossible to progress an action step beyond a certain point. You may be awaiting information, expecting a delivery or need to speak with someone who is not currently available. In cases like these you will want to get on with another action step and come back to the incomplete one later. In general, however, aim to see every action step through to completion before beginning something else. This is the most reliable way of ensuring that everything is completed, and that your timeline, project maps and so on reflect the true status of the project.

Create a project manual

Keep a project manual as you work through. This is a day-by-day summary of what you did and how it worked. By the time the project is complete, it will form an invaluable reference text for anyone managing a similar project in the future, and for yourself during your next project.

As well as providing practical information, the project manual is an additional way of ensuring that you stay on track, as you have to sit back and look objectively at what has been accomplished each day. It also ensures that you record your wins – the little triumphs that are quickly forgotten as you rush on to the next challenge. You may have persuaded a supplier to deliver 24 hours earlier than it said was possible, or had a chat with one of your team members that re-inspired them in the project.

The basic rule in deciding what goes into the project manual is to ask yourself: 'what happened today that would have been useful to know before I began this project?' This might range from crucial pieces of information, down to any little hints and tips you would pass on to someone else in the same position.

Take particular care to note anything unexpected – things that worked unexpectedly well, as well as things that went unexpectedly wrong. If you know why the reality differed from the theory, make a note of this also. If an action step took significantly more or less time than expected, note the scale of the discrepancy as well as the explanation – this will be invaluable in putting together future estimates. Similarly with cost items that finished significantly over- or underbudget; you will record the figures on your budget form, but make a note in the project manual of how it happened.

Note also any useful contacts you make during the project – you never know when they may be helpful again. If you are likely to forget the details of the conversation, you might like to jot down a few notes to remind yourself who they are and what role they played in case you do need to speak to them in future.

Keep a specific section in your project manual for acknowledgements. This is the place to make a note of all the people who helped you in some way, together with a brief note of what it was they did. This would include the occasions when your team members went above and beyond the call of duty, suppliers who provided outstanding service, colleagues who provided helpful advice and so on. You can then use this section to send 'thank you' letters or cards, either during a slack time in the project, or once the project is complete. People remember and appreciate this type of acknowledgement, so besides being a decent thing to do, it will also make them more likely to want to do a similar service for you should you need it in a future project.

SUMMARY

- Used effectively, paper can be a powerful aid to producing results; used ineffectively, it can drown a project.

- If you think you do not have time to organize your working environment, then you do not have time *not* to.

- Your in-tray is the source of all paperwork and is thus key to creating an effective paper management system. Use the prioritizing system covered in this chapter to eliminate useless paper and prioritize the rest.

- Put a permanent stop to unwanted materials by returning them with an instruction to delete you from the distribution list. Use computer-printed sticky labels to make this a ten-second task.

- Consider buying new office furniture if your existing office does not support you in working productively. The cost of even a top-quality system can be covered by just a two to five hours additional productive time per week.

- Organize your desk and furniture to suit your working patterns.

- Design your filing system to match the needs of the project. Remove irrelevant information, and turn your filing system into a colour-coded, active filing system.

- Take control of your incoming information by designing forms to be used by your project team. These forms will ensure that you have control over the nature, structure and quantity of information you receive.

- Update your project maps at least daily.

- Do not leave action steps incomplete unless it really cannot be helped. Part-complete actions risk delay, loss of momentum and prevent you working at peak efficiency.

- Create a project manual to record what you did, what worked and what did not work. Update it daily, noting anything you wish you had known before you started. Keep a special section to record exceptional contributions made to the project so that you can send 'thank you' letters or cards.

8

REMAINING SANE

or The job will not happen if the project manager cracks up

Imagine driving a car flat-out in fourth gear for 12 hours a day or more, throwing in a little bit of whatever fuel came to hand as and when you happened to think of it, giving no thought to maintenance and not even bothering to replenish the oil or water. We would be surprised if the car survived, let alone transported us to our destination on time.

Yet we often treat ourselves in a similar fashion – working long hours, eating the occasional sandwich or burger, having insufficient sleep, not taking any more exercise than the walk to the car each evening, and taking little or no time off to relax and have fun.

There are times, of course, when such a working pattern really is necessary. A major disaster, or unexpected opportunity, can justify working like this for a day or two. But anything longer than this is actually counterproductive: *countless studies have proven that working too hard means that you actually complete less effective work than if you work at a reasonable pace.* Although we each have our individual efficiency cycles – the times of the day when we are at our most creative and productive – the overall pattern is the same for each of us: we are at our most productive in the first few hours of work, with a second peak after a lunch break, and then grow gradually less effective throughout the day. After about ten hours, we are operating at something like 20 per cent efficiency. After 12 hours, we are lucky if we are at 10 per cent efficiency.

Think about this. A job performed at the end of a ten-hour day will take approximately five times as long, or be performed five times as poorly, as the same job left until nine o'clock the following morning. It does not take a mathematical genius to see that, once you *begin* working long hours, and suffering the resulting loss of efficiency, you will quickly become trapped into *continuing* to work long hours. Everything will begin to take longer and longer; the more time it takes, the more pressure you will feel and the longer you will work. The result is a rapidly descending spiral.

Once you are trapped in this spiral, escape appears impossible. There is just too much to do and too little time in which to do it. The idea that escape lies in working shorter hours seems illogical, and someone caught up in the spiral will often find the idea impossible even to consider – despite the fact that it has been proven time and time again.

This is the reason I called this chapter *Remaining sane*: this downward spiral is almost literally a form of insanity. You are behaving in a way which appears perfectly reasonable to you, yet is in direct conflict with the proven facts. This is a good working definition of insanity.

This insanity not only reduces your chances of completing the project to the required standard on time, it also places at risk your health, family life and general enjoyment of life.

There are five keys to retaining a sane working pattern:

- reasonable working hours;
- sufficient sleep;
- a nutritious diet;
- regular exercise;
- regular time off.

Working hours

> People are always blaming their circumstances for what they are. I do not believe in circumstance. The people who get on in life are the people who get up and look for the circumstances they want and, if they can't find them, make them.
>
> George Bernard Shaw

The eight-hour working day, with a one-hour lunch-break, has become the standard working day in most temperate climates for the simple reason that it works. It allows sufficient time to get the job done, and allows you to stop work before your efficiency drops to the point where any further work would be a waste of time.

As we saw in Chapter 6, an eight-hour working day probably gives you something like five hours of actual productive work on your project. Bear this in mind when scheduling work, and remember your declining efficiency: a full eight-hour workload equates to a true time of 12–13 hours by the time you have allowed for lunch, routine work, distractions and a rapidly diminishing efficiency rate.

If the nature of your work allows you to choose your own hours, notice whether you are a morning, afternoon or evening person. You might find that you work most efficiently by starting at 7 a.m. and going home at 3 p.m., or starting at 11 a.m. and working until 7 p.m., or even starting at 2 p.m. and working until 10 p.m. Working hours which avoid the rush hours also mean that you have a much more pleasant time travelling to and from work.

Of course, you need to be available to your team, suppliers, clients and so on, but even if you cannot work your ideal working hours, at least move towards them – even starting an hour earlier or later can make a big difference.

Recognize and use your peak hours

Pay attention to your ups and downs during the day. Most of us have a fairly consistent cycle of peaks and troughs. Notice when you feel at your most alert, and schedule your most demanding work accordingly. For example, you might notice a peak between 10 a.m. and noon, or between 3 p.m. and 5 p.m. Make good use of this peak period. Take steps to ensure that you will not be interrupted during this time. Ask your secretary to take messages (if you do not have a secretary, consider buying an answerphone and letting that answer your calls). Let your colleagues know that you are unavailable during those hours. Block off the time in your diary.

Most important of all, learn to recognize when you are no longer working efficiently. And be honest! There are times when we go through the motions because we think we *should* be able to keep going, but the truth is that we will usually end up doing it again properly the next day. When this happens, stop working and go home.

You may also notice times when you are not working effectively in the middle of the day. Take a 5–10 minute break. Have a coffee. Take a brisk walk outside. Close the door, take the 'phone off the hook and close your eyes for ten minutes. Read a few pages of a book. Make a phone call to a friend. Play a computer game. Bring in a personal stereo and listen to a favourite piece of music. Do anything that gives you a break and takes your mind off your work for a few minutes, allowing you to return to it afresh.

Working internationally

If you are working in a hot climate, it is generally a good idea to adopt the local working pattern. This might mean starting work early in the morning, to take advantage of the relative cool, with a three-hour siesta during the hottest part of the day, for example.

If much of your work is international, and you need to communicate across time zones, schedule phone calls for times when your working hours overlap so that neither party needs to stay late or take calls at home. There is a four-hour overlap in the working hours of London and New York, for example.

Where there is a very limited overlap, or no overlap at all (as between London and Sydney), use faxes and electronic mail messages rather than phone calls. This means that both parties can continue to work normal hours, while still allowing for daily communication. (See Chapter 9 for information on faxes and electronic mail.) Fax and E-mail have the added benefit of being a very much cheaper way to communicate internationally than conventional phone calls.

If your work involves a considerable amount of international travel, do not be tempted to succumb to the 'macho' image of someone unaffected by jet lag or stress. Jet lag affects us all, whether we notice the effects or not. When scheduling your trips, allow sufficient time to catch up on your sleep and adjust to the new time zone before you do any serious work. You can cost your company more money in a single jet-lagged negotiation than you will save in a whole year of cutting your out-of-office time to the bone.

Sleep

We all need different amounts of sleep. Some people manage very happily on four hours, while others need seven, eight or nine. A good way to find out how much sleep you really need is to pick a time when you do not have to be up early the following morning (at a weekend, for example), note what time you go to bed and then allow yourself to wake naturally in the morning – no alarm clocks, no kids rushing in, nothing! Try that a few times, and you will almost certainly find that you average about the same number of hours each time. (This will not work, obviously, if you are particularly tired because you have just finished a 90-hour week!)

Once you know how much sleep you need, schedule it: calculate what time you need to go to bed to allow for this amount of sleep. Aim to get your natural sleeping time at least five nights out of seven.

Again, there will always be emergencies (and parties!) that result in less sleep for a night or two. The important thing is to ensure that it does not become a habit: lack of sleep results in a similar downward spiral to long working hours.

And do not rely on weekends to catch up on your sleep. You need time for relaxation (not the same as sleep), your family and leisure activities as well as sleep.

Food

Not eating enough, or eating only snacks, is usually part of the same pattern as working long hours. When you constantly feel under pressure, that there is not enough time to complete all your tasks, eating becomes a luxury, something you will get around to when you have done everything else.

The human body is no different from any other machine: it cannot work effectively without a good fuel supply. An occasional sandwich and a Mars bar, washed down with a half-cold cup of vending-machine coffee, does not constitute a good fuel supply.

We have already discussed the decline in efficiency during a working day. The position is far worse if you do not take a lunch break. Instead of the usual second efficiency peak in the afternoon, followed by a decline towards the end of the day, your efficiency drops steadily from about 11 a.m., falling to 20 per cent by early afternoon, rather than by 6–7 p.m.

Similarly with skipping breakfast and dinner, both symptoms of an overlong, overstressed working day. Your body does not have the fuel it needs to begin the day effectively, so your efficiency not only declines at a faster rate, it starts out lower in the first place.

Again, there will always be emergencies when you need to skip a meal. But if it becomes a habit, your overall productivity will drop dramatically, and you enter the same downward spiral.

Exercise

If you do not believe there is any correlation between exercise and mental efficiency, try a simple test. Next time you find yourself stuck with a difficult problem, go outside for a gentle 10-minute jog. You do not need to set any Olympic records, or come back to the office drenched in sweat, you need only jog gently at a pace just fast enough that you can feel your heartbeat. Now return to the problem.

A quick jog does not guarantee you any miraculous insights, of course, but it does increase the oxygen supply to the brain (as well as to your whole body), which results in clearer thinking.

Regular exercise strengthens the heart muscles which not only means that you are able to do more physical work for less effort, it also means that your heart works more efficiently when your body is at rest – including when you are sitting at your desk working.

The generally recommended minimum exercise schedule to ensure health and fitness is twenty minutes aerobic exercise three times a week. Aerobic simply means that your heartbeat reaches a certain range for the 20-minute period. This range is calculated as follows:

1. Subtract your age from 220.
2. Multiply this figure by 0.6 for the minimum heartbeat.
3. Multiply the same figure by 0.8 for the maximum heartbeat.

The resulting figures are in heartbeats per minute. Let us take an example. Suppose that you are aged 35:

1. 220-35 = 185.
2. 185 x 0.6 = 111 (minimum heartbeats per minute).
3. 185 x 0.8 = 148 (maximum heartbeats per minute).

So, you are exercising aerobically any time your heartbeat is in the range 111–148 beats per minute for a continuous period of 20 minutes or more.

You can easily check this during exercise by dividing the above figures by six to give you the number of heartbeats in a ten-second period. You can then take your pulse for ten seconds during your exercise.

Note that it is as important not to exceed the maximum figure as it is to reach the minimum. A heartbeat above your maximum aerobic rate is what fitness experts call *anaerobic* and can actually be harmful.

Typical aerobic exercises include running, cycling (fairly hard), rowing, swimming and dancing. Note that exercise is only aerobic if it is *continuous* for at least 20 minutes.

Again, the temptation is to argue that you do not have enough time to exercise. In practice, however, your increased productivity – not to mention feeling of vitality – will more than cancel out the time it takes to exercise for an hour a week. Failure to exercise, however, results in our old friend the downward spiral. *Warning: Do consult your doctor before beginning any exercise programme, especially if you are over 40 years old.*

Time off

Time off means two things: time to relax, and time to engage in leisure activities. Note that relaxation does not mean sleep – you should have time simply to enjoy restful activities in addition to getting enough sleep.

Relaxing activities typically include reading, listening to music, talking with family and friends, playing with children (sometimes!), gardening, watching TV, meals out and so on. All that matters is to choose something that enables you to forget about work and enjoy yourself in a restful way.

If you also enjoy an active pursuit, all the better. It has been shown that the most refreshing break includes a mixture of relaxing activities and an active pursuit – something that demands both physical and mental skills. Examples include most sports (squash, tennis, cricket, football, badminton and so on) as well as outdoor pursuits like sailing and climbing. A weekend in which one day is spent relaxing at home, and the other engaged in an active sport or hobby, can be as refreshing as a short holiday.

Two further tips for remaining sane

First, remain in control of the project! While you should welcome constructive suggestions and specialist advice, there are some projects where everyone and his grandmother will have some advice to dispense. Consider all the advice you can usefully implement, but remember that in the final analysis it is your project, and you need to work the way that suits you and your team.

Treat this book in the same way. Everything it contains has been proven to work for others, but what matters is to do what works best for *you*. If any of the advice in this book (after you have tried it!) does not work for you and your project, ignore it.

Second, find yourself a buddy! A project buddy is a friend who is willing to be a sounding post and a sympathetic ear for you throughout the project. It should ideally be someone outside the organization, but certainly someone who is not involved in your project.

A buddy is someone you can moan to when nothing is going right. Someone you can bounce ideas off before you try them on your team. Someone who will check that you are taking care of your health and well-being. And – ideally – the kind of friend you can phone at 4 a.m. if you wake up in the middle of the night with a sudden panic about the project!

When choosing a buddy, check that they have the time available to perform this function. Some people like to have a 10-minute conversation with their buddy at the beginning and end of each day, as well as any 'emergency' calls that may be needed at other times. It needs to be a friend who will keep you calm and restore your sense of humour. And who will not give you abundant unwanted advice when all you really want is someone to sympathize and help put you in a suitable frame of mind to launch yourself back into the fray!

Your first duty is to survive!

It may be an exaggeration to say 'take care of yourself and the project will take care of itself', but there is also a great deal of truth in it. The project will not succeed if you do not remain sane throughout the time it takes to complete it, so your first duty is to take care of your own well-being. It does not matter how many urgent things need to be done; if you are not in a fit state to work effectively, correcting that needs to be your number one priority. Always.

SUMMARY

- We would not dream of driving a car the way we drive ourselves, yet our bodies need fuel, rest and maintenance every bit as much as a car.

- Studies have shown that working longer than average hours on a regular basis actually *reduces* our productivity.

- Our efficiency drops off markedly towards the end of the day. After ten hours, we are working at 20 per cent efficiency, which means that tasks will either take five times longer than if you left them until tomorrow, or the quality will be five times poorer.

- Once you start working long hours, your reduced efficiency will mean that the job as a whole takes longer and longer, and you are forced into a downward spiral of ever longer hours.

- The solution is to *reduce* your working hours to a reasonable level and thus improve your efficiency; however, to someone trapped in the downward spiral, this will seem like the last thing they need to do.

- Consistently working long hours not only reduces your efficiency, it also places at risk your health, family life and general enjoyment of life.

- To maximize your effectiveness, work no more than eight hours a day.

- If you can choose your own working hours, notice whether you work most effectively in the morning, afternoon or evening, and adjust your working hours to suit.

- Pay attention to your peaks and troughs during the day; most people have consistent patterns, giving peak performance at particular hours of the day. Plan your most demanding work for these hours, and ensure this time is uninterrupted.

- Recognize when you are no longer working efficiently and stop work at this point.

- If you lose concentration in the middle of the day, take a 5–10 minute break.

- If the need to communicate across time zones keeps you at the office late, or means taking business calls at home, use fax and electronic mail as much as possible so that both parties can work normal hours while maintaining daily communication.

- Find out how much sleep you need and schedule this much sleep at least five nights out of seven.

- Do not skip meals. Skipping lunch means your efficiency drops to 20 per cent as early as 3–4 p.m., and skipping breakfast or dinner means that your efficiency still drops at the same rate but begins at a lower level.

- Follow a programme of aerobic exercise (as defined in this chapter): at least 20 minutes a day, three times a week.

- Schedule time off for both relaxation (not just sleep) and active pursuits such as sports.

- Welcome advice, but work the way that suits you and your team.

- Find yourself a project buddy!

9

AVOIDING THE TECHNOLOGY TRAP

or Open the pod door, Hal . . .

Using technology effectively can boost your productivity – or reduce your costs – by several hundred per cent. It can free you from boring and repetitive tasks, give you closer control over your projects, improve the accuracy of your work, enable more flexible working patterns and accelerate your responsiveness. It would be folly to fail to take advantage of these benefits. Indeed, there are projects, even businesses, which would not even be feasible without access to the appropriate technology.

The delights of modern technology, however, are such that it is very easy to fall into what I call the technology trap. The trap is to adopt new technology unthinkingly, taking the view that a hi-tech solution is automatically better than a low-tech one.

I have fallen into the technology trap myself. When electronic diaries first became available, I immediately went out and bought one. The benefits seemed indisputable: it could hold all my appointments in a tiny pocket-sized unit, I could search for a particular appointment or action, I did not have to buy refills, it would sound an alarm when I needed to be somewhere . . . and yet the simple fact is that it turned out to be far less effective than my paper-based system. The tiny screen meant that I could not get a proper overview of my week. It was actually slower to type search details into the electronic unit than to flip through the pages of my paper diary. Completed items did not stand out sufficiently from incomplete ones. I could not simply make a photocopy of my schedule for a colleague. And so on. Not only was the electronic diary a waste of money, it also cost me a substantial amount of time (even ignoring the time lost when someone dropped my jacket on the ground, smashing the screen and putting the unit out of action for a week!).

There are numerous other examples of technological 'aids' which require you to invest more time and money than they will ever save.

To help you through the maze, this chapter discusses some of the main forms of technology you might consider. It is divided into three sections: *Must have, Don't touch*, and *Consider*.

The *Must have* section lists those items of technology that I consider useful for *any* type of project, and where the benefit far outweighs the cost. These are items without which I would not even begin a project.

The *Consider* section lists items that may be useful, depending on the your needs.

The *Don't touch* section lists one item of technology I would actively discourage you from using. I mention it only because it would seem a logical purchase: project management software.

All my comments are based on personal experience – I do not write about anything I have not used – but remember: the acid test, as always, is to find out what works for you.

Wherever possible, try before you buy. See if the supplier will lend you a demonstration unit before you commit yourself; if the benefits really are as great as the company claims, it should be happy to arrange this. Failing this, insist on an extensive demonstration, with enough time to experiment on your own, and talk to other users about their experiences with the equipment.

It is beyond the scope of this book to discuss particular makes and models of equipment, but you will find a wide range of magazines carrying reviews of specific equipment. Again, take the views of the reviewer into account, but always try the equipment for yourself to evaluate how useful it would be to *you*.

I have taken as read that you already use personal computers with standard business software like wordprocessors, databases, spreadsheets and so on. If you do not, then the detailed advice needed is beyond the scope of a brief chapter in this book, but I do recommend that you take a look at a few up-to-date books covering the pros and cons of buying a personal computer.

The golden rule

There is one golden rule when evaluating any business aid, technological or otherwise. Ask yourself the following question: Will it save me time, money or effort? If the answer is yes, and the saving is sufficient to justify the investment, go ahead; if the answer is no, forget it – no matter how clever, impressive or pretty it may be.

This golden rule requires two caveats.

1. Remember to take into account the impact the technology may have on the 'soft' factors like staff morale. As we saw in Chapter 1, so-called soft factors have hard financial worth. A good-quality coffee machine may appear to offer no direct benefit to the effectiveness of the business, but – if it makes your staff feel that the organization appreciates them and cares about their working environment – it is likely to deliver excellent value for money through improved productivity and quality of work. Failing to consider soft factors is characteristic of the 'short-sighted accountant' mentality that begins by stripping a company of cost items, and ends up stripping it of its best employees.

2. Be prepared for an initial investment of time. Every piece of technology has a learning curve, during which the benefits may be negligible. You thus have to evaluate the eventual benefits against the initial investment of time required. A substantial eventual benefit will justify a relatively long learning curve; a smaller end-benefit will only justify a shorter learning curve.

Must have

Hands-free memory phone

A hands-free phone is a telephone which allows you to hold a telephone conversation without lifting the handset, thus leaving your hands free for other tasks like taking notes or using a computer. A memory phone is a telephone handset which stores telephone numbers and will dial them for you automatically at the touch of a button or two. Put the two together and you have a telephone unit that allows you to make and receive calls with maximum ease and minimum inconvenience.

The average manager spends more than an hour a day on the phone. Based on an 8-hour day, that works out to almost a month and a half each year! Anything you can do to make this time more productive has to be worthwhile.

Speakerphones are particularly useful if you do not have a full-time secretary. Rather than hanging on to a handset waiting for the other person to pick up the phone, you can just set the phone dialling and get on with something else until you hear them answer. Being put on hold is no longer the same frustrating experience – simply carry on with other work until the call is connected.

They are also useful when you need to take notes, particularly if you want to type details straight into a personal computer: you can use both hands to type, thus dramatically increasing your typing speed and reducing the length of the call.

Speakerphones are also invaluable if you want two or three people to take part in a telephone conversation – most good-quality handsets enable three people to hear and be heard with ease. This type of 'mini conference call' can be extremely effective in reaching rapid decisions when several people need to be consulted.

Memory phones typically store anything from 10 to 50 telephone numbers. The most useful type to buy is a one with 'direct input' memories – this means that you have a button alongside each name; to call that person, you just press the speakerphone button (or lift the handset) and then press a single button. The other type requires you to look up a one- or two-digit code, and press three or four buttons; these do not save much time really.

By programming your phone with your most frequently-called contacts, you can call them by just pressing a couple of buttons. You save the time it would have taken you to look up the number, and are safeguarded against accidentally dialling the wrong number.

A phone with 40 direct-input memories will be more than adequate for all your regular contacts, and will cost somewhere in the region of £50–80. If you spend a great deal of time on the phone, you may like to consider one of the much more sophisticated 'executive' phones which can store 200+ phone numbers and include a full QWERTY keyboard to allow you to enter their names. These typically cost upwards of £200. They also take up a significant amount of desk space.

One word of warning about any form of memory phone: do not store confidential telephone numbers or – worse – PIN numbers in the memories. If you store a telephone number and PIN number for a telebanking service, for example, anyone using your phone could access your bank account!

Fax machine

It seems rare these days to find an organization that does not have a fax machine, so why give a special mention to them here? For the simple reason that it is possible to make much greater use of them than most people do.

Most people still think of post as the standard way to send a letter or document, and fax as a backup to be used only when really needed. In fact, we would be better off reversing these options, and using fax as our standard method of communication, and resorting to the post only when there is a specific reason to do so – when sending goods, bulky documents, original artwork or contracts, for example. For one-page letters, fax is faster, cheaper and involves less effort.

Fax can also be used in place of many telephone conversations. Phone conversations are time-consuming, intrusive and open to misunderstandings. Faxed communications are much faster (about five minutes to draft and fax information that would take 20 minutes or more to convey by phone), do not interrupt the recipient and guarantee that the information received is the same as the information sent, not somebody's understanding or interpretation of what you said. And, of course, we have already mentioned the use of fax machines to overcome time differences in international communication.

Whenever you are about to make a telephone call, ask yourself whether you really need to make the call: would a fax do instead? Most modern machines include 50- or 100-number memories, so sending a fax is simply a matter of pressing a few buttons.

If you do not have a secretary to handle your faxes for you, the fax machine is constantly in use or you have to walk a long way to reach it, consider buying a fax machine for your own desk. This is not as extravagant as it may sound – you can buy a desktop fax machine for less than £300, and it will take up less space on your desk than a desk diary. Most desktop machines can share a phone line with a direct-dial telephone line, and you can buy a £100 'fax splitter' that will automatically send incoming calls to either the fax machine or your phone as appropriate.

If you have to handle a great deal of internal correspondence, consider connecting desktop fax machines to PABX extensions and faxing the information to colleagues. Since calls are routed through the in-house switchboard, calls are free and you can exchange written documents in seconds without leaving your desk.

One word of warning, however: the legal status of faxes is unclear in most countries. By all means send draft contracts by fax, to speed up the process of reaching agreement, but always send the final version by registered post. Similarly with other important documents. In my own company, for example, we frequently issue purchase orders, invoices and so on by fax, but always confirm them by putting a copy in the post.

Electronic organizer (for telephone numbers)

Pocket electronic organizers are calculator-style gadgets with miniature QWERTY keyboards that store telephone numbers, brief notes and schedules. As electronic diaries, I most definitely *do not* recommend them for the reasons explained earlier. For storing telephone numbers, however, they are invaluable.

You will, of course, have your most frequently-called numbers programmed into your memory phone. The organizer is for storing the rest, and for providing access to your regular numbers when you are out of the office or simply away from your desk.

A unit with a 64 k memory will store some two thousand telephone numbers, so it is unlikely you will ever run out of memory capacity. Buy one with a proper 'moving' keyboard, rather than the flat 'membrane' keyboard used on the cheaper machines. If possible, buy one that will dial the telephone numbers for you: they work by playing multi-frequency tones through a speaker which you hold over the telephone mouthpiece. This does not work on all telephone lines, but works on most PABX systems, most payphones, all cellular phones and any phone connected to a digital telephone exchange. At the time of writing, however, this facility was only available on the cheaper units which did not offer QWERTY keyboards and could store only 20–100 telephone numbers.

Most electronic organizers are small enough to slip easily into a shirt pocket or the smallest of handbags, and enable you to carry all your telephone numbers with you wherever you may be.

Microcassette recorder

A microcassette recorder is a pocket-sized cassette recorder which uses minute cassette tapes. They contain a built-in microphone, so recording a message is simply a matter of pressing a couple of buttons and holding the unit as you would a microphone.

The recorders themselves vary in size from something which fits a jacket pocket down to tiny, lightweight units that you can carry unobtrusively in the smallest pocket or bag. Generally speaking, the smaller and lighter the recorder, the higher the price. Prices range from less than £40 right up to £200+. A good-quality unit will cost between £100 and £120.

Microcassette recorders can be used for dictation, with your secretary playing the tapes on a desktop dictaphone machine, but are equally useful if you do not have a secretary just for making notes to yourself. Instead of having to find pen and paper, you can simply record a brief spoken message to yourself which you can replay on your return to the office.

They are especially useful when it would be inconvenient or impossible to use pen and paper. You can keep it on the dashboard when you are driving, for example; if inspiration strikes, or you simply want to make sure you do not forget something, you can quickly flick it on to record and then record your message while you keep both hands on the wheel. I also keep mine on my bedside table at night; that way, if I wake up at 3 a.m. with a sudden idea, I do not have to wake my wife by switching on a light – I just record a softly spoken message into the machine.

Microcassette recorders are also useful for recording meetings. I often record client briefings so that I can be sure I have a complete record of what was said, and can expand on my notes later if I am unsure of a point. Such recordings are also useful in case of a later dispute over what was said: though they are not accepted in court as evidence, the simple existence of a tape offers a degree of protection. I once completed some work for a client who later tried to avoid payment by claiming that he had given me totally different instructions. When I reminded him of my tape recording of our meeting, the cheque arrived the next day.

Many units offer a dual-speed motor. At the normal setting, you can record 30 minutes per side, making an hour per tape. At the slower speed, you can record two hours per tape at the expense of a slight drop in sound quality, so even a long meeting can be recorded on a single tape.

Cellphone

Probably the most controversial item on my *Must have* list! People seem to either love or hate them. Personally, I would not be without mine. It has saved me making unnecessary journeys, enabled me to solve potential crises on the spot, brought my company business we might otherwise have lost, repeatedly kept projects on time because suppliers and colleagues were able to reach me immediately, and – more than once – enabled me to make a 999 call within seconds rather than minutes of an emergency.

There are three basic types of cellphone: mobile (fitted to a car), transportable (carried like a small briefcase) and portable (small enough to be carried in a jacket pocket). Your choice of phone will depend largely on your working patterns. If all of your travelling is done by car, a mobile is appropriate as it offers the most reliable service and enables you to make and receive calls while driving without taking your hands off the steering wheel for more than a moment or two. Transportables are useful if you need portability but work in an environment where equipment needs to be tough – building sites, farms and so on. And portables are best when you do a lot of travelling by train, or spend a lot of time out of your car.

Cellphones offer two main benefits.

1. You can be contacted immediately in an emergency. This is vital if you, as the project manager, are out of the office when an unforeseen disaster strikes the project or a rapid decision has to be made. Your team members can call you, obtain advice or authority right away and the project can proceed without delay. And it can be extremely useful for you to have the same ability to call your team members when they are out of the office.

2. You can make urgent calls while you are on the move. This is useful both when you suddenly remember something important as your train pulls out of the station, and when you have been stuck in a traffic jam for half an hour and are going to be late for your meeting.

People are rightly concerned about the costs of running a cellphone. They are expensive, it has to be admitted. At the time of writing, calls within the London area cost 33p per minute. But the nature of urgent calls mean that they tend to be brief, averaging two or three minutes, and almost invariably save much more than they cost. And you can have an itemized bill, showing the date, time, duration, cost and phone number of every call made on the phone, enabling you to prevent abuse of the facility.

The other concern people have about cellphones is a fear of being disturbed by unwanted calls. This, however, is a needless concern: first, cellphone numbers are not listed in telephone directories or on the directory enquiries computer: it is up to you to give the number to people. You thus have complete control over who can and cannot reach you. And second, you can switch your phone off when you do not want to be disturbed, allowing your calls to be transferred to a message service instead.

Consider

Radiopager

If you really cannot bring yourself to use a cellphone, or cannot justify the cost for everyone on your team who spends time away from the office, the next best thing is a radiopager.

A radiopager is a miniature radio receiver which alerts you when somebody is trying to reach you. Again, there are three main types. The most basic type is called a tone pager. This simply bleeps when signalled, and you call your office to find out who called. Next is a numeric pager, which displays the telephone number and extension of the person trying to reach you. This is more convenient than a tone pager, since you do not have to call your office before you can return the call, but you still have to find a phone and make a phone call before you know what the message is. Most sophisticated of the three types is a message pager. This displays written messages of up to about 20 words – more on the top models. This enables you to receive the message straight away, and you only have to return the call if you need more information.

All three types are available for purchase or hire from a variety of suppliers. You also pay a monthly fee for the service itself. Costs vary from about £15 a month for a tone pager up to about £40 a month for the most sophisticated message pager.

Many pagers offer a silent option for times when you do not want to be disturbed – during an important meeting or presentation, for example. The pager then flashes a light or vibrates gently to alert you to an incoming message. This can make them less obtrusive than cellphones for times when you cannot answer a call, but would still like to be able to receive messages.

Laptop computer

If you rely on a computer for much of your work, and spend a fair amount of 'dead' time outside the office – on planes and trains, for example – a laptop computer can have a phenomenal impact on your productivity. They are especially valuable if you make frequent trips abroad, enabling you to turn a hotel room into a temporary office.

There seem to be three main types of most forms of technology, and laptop computers are no exception. At the bottom end are simple 'notebook' computers. These are generally small, light and relatively inexpensive, but do not offer full computing facilities. They are primarily intended for wordprocessing – writing reports, memos, letters and so on – but usually also include 'organizer' functions like an electronic diary, card index, calculator and so on. Most are also suitable for use with electronic mail services (see below). Notebook computers range in price from about £300 to £800.

Next come basic PC-compatible laptops. These run the main IBM-compatible software packages, but do not offer the speed, memory or hard disk capacity of a desktop machine. They generally allow you to use your usual software, but are slower and do not allow you to carry all your files with you. Basic PC-compatible laptops cost around £1 000.

Finally come full-power laptops. These offer all the power and storage capacity of a desktop computer, but in a portable unit. You can use one of these as your main desktop machine, and then simply take it with you when you want to be able to work on the move. The price varies tremendously, depending on the exact specification, but start at about £1 500 and rise to over £6 000.

Beware of one particular class of full-power laptops. These look exactly like standard portable computers, but require mains power. They are fine if you simply want to be able to use your computer in two different offices, or at work and at home, but do not, of course, allow you to work while on the move – on planes, for example.

(Incidentally, you would be surprised at the number of places where you will find power sockets – on trains, in parks and so on – but this is very cheeky and not very reliable, even if you would use less than a penny's worth of electricity in an hour. In the days before battery-powered computers, I approached British Rail and suggested that it made power sockets available in InterCity carriages. I received a decidedly curt letter, which a friendly railway engineer assured me was total nonsense, but decided that it was not worth the fight.)

Your choice of laptop will depend on the type of work you need to do. If you are away for several days at a time, and rely heavily on a computer, a full-power laptop is probably worth the expense. If you need to run standard PC software, but are only out of the office for a few hours at a time, a basic PC-compatible laptop will probably do the trick. And if you only need the ability to write while you are on the move, and perhaps access an electronic mail service, a notebook laptop will be sufficient. If a notebook computer is sufficient, you will have the benefit of a machine that is smaller and lighter than most laptops, and offers a substantially longer battery life.

Bear in mind that choosing a computer is an important decision, and you should seek advice from your in-house information technology manager or an independent dealer before making your choice. These notes are merely intended to steer you in the right general direction.

Three special points for frequent travellers are worth bearing in mind:

1. While most airlines are happy to allow the use of laptop computers during a flight, one or two consider them a hazard to navigation equipment on board the aircraft, and thus ban their use. (The rationale is that laptop computers can cause radio interference, but this seems rather far-fetched in practice since the radius of any such interference extends only a centimetre or two beyond the computer's casing, and is in any case very weak.) You are usually allowed to take them into the cabin, but are not allowed to switch them on during the flight. This applies only to a mere handful of the world's airlines.

2. Some airport security checkpoints like to take a very careful look at portable computers which can, in extreme cases, delay you sufficiently to miss a flight. This happened to me once at Frankfurt airport, shortly after the Lockerbie disaster, when the security staff subjected it to a whole variety of tests lasting almost an hour and a half, and then insisted that it travel in the pressurized section of the hold. This was the only occasion,

however, that a security check has caused me to miss a flight in seven years of carrying a laptop with me on every business trip I have made.

Finally, do not allow your laptop to go through one of the old-style X-ray machines used at some smaller airports. The modern machines used at major international business airports are perfectly safe, but some older machines emit powerful magnetic fields which can erase data from the machine, so always insist on a manual check if you have any doubts.

Electronic mail

Electronic mail is the modern alternative to telex. It allows you to send and receive written messages using a computer – desktop or laptop – over an ordinary telephone line.

Electronic mail offers all the benefits of fax, with one main advantage: it operates independent of your location. Instead of your messages being sent to a fixed destination, they are held in a central computer system until you collect them. You collect your messages by using your computer to connect to the electronic mail service over an ordinary telephone line, and can collect your messages from Edinburgh, Amsterdam or New York as easily as from your own office.

This ability to send and receive messages from any telephone, anywhere in the world (even a payphone, with the right equipment) makes electronic mail the perfect means of communication for frequent travellers using laptop computers. One company director who spends two weeks a month travelling uses electronic mail to receive memos and reports forwarded by his secretary. He sends back his instructions the following day, together with correspondence which his secretary prints on to letterheads and posts. This enables him to remain fully in touch with the business, and give his secretary an even workload, without having to worry about different time zones.

Another advantage of electronic mail is that documents sent to you can be loaded directly into your computer. Reports can be edited in your wordprocessor, printed and passed on. Financial data can be loaded into a spreadsheet or accounts package for analysis. Names and addresses can be loaded directly into a marketing database. And so on.

There are a number of competing electronic mail services in most developed countries. Again, obtain advice from your information technology manager, or consult the computer press (most computer dealers, unfortunately, know very little about electronic mail).

Telephone conference calls

Telephone conference calls enable people at three or more different locations to take part in the same telephone conversation: it is effectively a meeting held over the phone.

The main benefit of conference calls is that you can hold a 'meeting' with people in widely scattered locations without the cost, inconvenience and lost time involved in everyone travelling to a single venue. A conference call lasting one hour, and involving people at ten different locations within a single country, will cost around £200. Compare this to the cost of bringing all those people together and immediately you can see the benefits. International conference calls are more expensive, but the relative savings are even higher.

The main disadvantage of a telephone conference call is the lack of visual information. Not only can you not see the person talking, but the speaker cannot point to graphs, tables and other visual information. This disadvantage can be partly overcome by careful preparation: you can fax copies of any visual aids to the participants before the conference call begins.

Conference calls are particularly effective when you need to give a project update and/or morale-boosting pep-talk to a dispersed team, being a good way to generate a sense of a national or international team pulling together for the same end. It is, however, vital to plan your conference calls carefully. You need an agenda, which everyone has in front of them, and a chairperson to keep the 'meeting' in order and decide who will speak at any one time. It is also a good idea to ask people to phone in five or ten minutes before the call is due to start to allow time for everyone to be connected, and to take a roll-call at the beginning of the call to ensure that everyone is there.

Contact your telephone company for details.

Videoconferencing

A videoconference is the closest thing you can have to a meeting without everyone physically travelling to a central venue.

Until a few years ago, videoconferences were the domain of a handful of multinationals with private studios. Today, however, anyone can hire a public studio by the hour. There are public videoconferencing studios in most of the world's large business centres.

Most studios are designed for a maximum of six people per location. Any more than this, and it becomes difficult to see and hear people clearly. A standard videoconference takes place between two locations, and the participants can see and hear each other at all times – this is just like a normal meeting. You can, however, set up three-way links, with the chairperson controlling who talks at any one time.

The quality of modern videoconferencing systems has to be seen to be believed. The usual arrangement is that you sit at a desk, facing a large colour screen. The other studio will typically be furnished and laid out in an identical fashion, giving a convincing illusion of everyone being in the same room. The quality of the pictures in a 'full blown' videoconferencing studio is much higher than even the best television sets; you can easily see small details of facial expression. The sound quality is also extremely lifelike, and I find that I quickly forget that it is a videoconference and treat it just like any other meeting. The illusion is so strong that it seems strange when you cannot stand up and walk along the corridor with someone after the meeting!

Most studios are equipped with the usual range of visual aids, including an overhead projector and whiteboard, which can be seen at the other end. There is also a separate camera designed to allow those at the other end to examine documents, models, components and so on. The camera can be zoomed in to show fine detail, and the resolution is so good that computer engineers can identify faults in a printed circuit board by studying the transmitted image.

If I seem enthusiastic about videoconferencing, it is because I am: I became a firm convert the first time I ever took part in a videoconference.

As you might expect, videoconferences are not cheap but, again, costs compare very favourably indeed to the costs of bring everyone together. An hour-long videoconference linking two studios in the same country costs about £300 per hour, while the same one-hour conference between London and New York would cost about £2 500. This seems expensive until you consider that the expenses alone of sending just one person across the Atlantic business class, with a couple of nights' accommodation at a standard business hotel, will easily exceed this figure, and the true cost – taking into account the fact that two whole days are lost in travel – is far higher.

You do, however, have to allow a certain amount of travel time for a videoconference. Unless your organization is fortunate enough to have an in-house studio, participants will have to travel to and from the nearest public studio. This is unlikely to exceed 30 minutes each way if you are based in a large city centre.

Electronic diary software

You can buy electronic diary software for most desktop and laptop computers. Such software usually handles your schedule, action list and reminders such as birthdays and anniversaries.

Most software handles both appointments and action lists. So far as appointments are concerned, it will typically allow you to enter, delete and edit appointment details; search for a particular person or company, to find out when you are scheduled to meet; and search for a free slot (you tell it that you want to meet with somebody for three hours, and it will find the first free three-hour slot). This latter feature is of limited use as it does not usually check your action lists, so it may well identify days on which you are too busy to accept *any* appointments.

Diary software will normally allow you to print out sections of your diary, if you need them while you are out of the office, but if you schedule appointments while you are away from your computer, you have the danger of storing appointment details in two places: the version in your computer, and additional details handwritten on a printout. This is fine as long as you discipline yourself to transfer the details to your computer as soon as you return to the office. You will inevitably miss appointments if you forget to do so.

The problem does not arise if you use a laptop computer which you carry with you. You can then enter appointments directly into the computer.

Action lists are normally held in a separate section on the screen. The main benefit of computerizing such lists is that the software will allow you to sort them into order of priority, and will automatically carry forward actions which you have not completed by the end of the day.

Storing action lists on a computer has two main disadvantages. One is that the space available for actions may be limited – some software displays only ten actions at a time, for example. The other is that completed actions are often marked only with a small symbol, making it difficult to see at a glance what you have already achieved and what still remains to be done.

It is essential, with any electronic diary system, to ensure that it is memory-resident; that is, that you can access your diary even when you are already using the computer for something else. There is nothing more frustrating, or damaging to your productivity, to have to stop work, close your document and load a new piece of software just to check your diary or update your action list.

Make sure, too, that the software allows you to create backup copies of your diary on floppy disk, especially if you use a laptop computer, and discipline yourself to make daily backups: the worst that can happen if you drop a paper diary on to the floor is that you have to put the pages back into the binder. Drop a laptop computer on the floor, and you will probably lose all the data on the hard disk – including your appointment details.

A system which enables you to take regular backups is actually more secure than a paper system, as you still have your appointment details if the computer is lost or stolen.

If you do decide to use PC diary software, it is wise to run in parallel with your paper-based system for two or three weeks. While it is irritating having to write things in two different places, it is not nearly so irritating as finding out the hard way that your electronic diary does not work in quite the way you thought it did and losing all your appointments!

Don't touch

Project management software

Project management software designed for personal computers is, in my view, a classic example of the technology trap.

If you have a project to manage, and a PC on your desk, buying project management software seems a most logical step. The purchase cost is not excessive – somewhere in the region of £300–500 – and there is no disputing the fact that most of the packages available look extremely impressive. Such packages will automatically calculate the time needed to complete a project, compute the critical path and the slack time in each of the remaining paths, integrate the project budget into the timeline, highlight clashes in personnel or resources, instantly show the effect of any delay or acceleration in the project ... and on and on. When I first read a description like this, I could not wait to get my hands on such a package.

The reality is a bitter disappointment. Yes, such packages do offer all the facilities listed. But the way in which they work means that they offer few benefits over a manual system, and they take *much* longer to set up and use.

Creating a timeline in a project management package takes five to ten times as long as creating the same timeline manually. This could be justified if the package was that much faster to use once the project is underway. This just is not the case. The software *does* automatically perform calculations for you, of course, and will point out scheduling conflicts or imminent delays, but much of the work required in telling the software how to resolve these conflicts is actually more trouble than doing so manually, and – when the software *does* handle something automatically, it usually does not tell you exactly what it has done, so you have manually to compare the new timeline with the previous version to find out what changes are required.

PC-based systems also fall down in a basic fashion. For a timeline to be truly effective, it has to be displayed in a place where everyone involved can refer to it. A PC does not satisfy this need. To have to load software on a PC, and scroll the timeline across a relatively small screen, just is not feasible and, unless you have an A1 colour plotter available, printing out a new version each day would take you about an hour – you have to sellotape together lots and lots of pieces of A4 paper in the right order!

There are much more sophisticated project management packages available on minicomputers and mainframes, and these can be vital for extremely complex projects like the design and construction of a new aircraft, but PC-based project management software really is more hype than performance.

Take a look at it for yourself by all means, but please take a very thorough look before you consider entrusting your project to such software. My advice, as I say, is do not touch it.

SUMMARY

- Using appropriate technology offers so many benefits, it would be foolhardy to ignore them.

- Beware the technology trap: investing more time and money in inappropriate technology than you will ever recoup.

- The golden rule when evaluating new technology is to ask yourself whether it will save you time, money or effort; if the answer is yes, and the saving is sufficient to justify the investment, go ahead; otherwise, leave well alone no matter how clever, impressive or pretty it may be.

- The golden rule has two caveats: remember to consider the impact on so-called 'soft' factors like staff morale, and be prepared for the initial investment of time required in the early stages of the learning curve.

- My *Must have* technology for project management includes a hands-free memory phone, fax machine, electronic organizer (for storing phone numbers, *not* your schedule), a microcassette recorder and a cellphone.

- Fax machines can be far more useful than we think. Read my suggestions in this chapter for details.

- My *Consider* technology includes a radiopager, laptop computer, electronic mail, telephone conference calls, videoconferencing and PC diary software.

- Do not touch project management software: it is less efficient than manual methods.

10

CRISIS PROJECTS

or The Chairman wants it by 4 p.m. tomorrow

This chapter details a proven approach to crisis management. In keeping with the need for speed, I have kept it deliberately brief and to the point. Take the time to read it *before* a crisis arises, and simply skim quickly through it to refresh your memory once the crisis strikes. While you cannot always prepare for the individual crisis in question, you *can* take steps to ensure that you are in a position to respond rapidly to crises in general.

Since there are organizations in which *every* project appears to be a crisis project, I will start by defining what I mean by a crisis project. *A crisis project is one where the result has to be produced in a week or less, where commonsense suggests that it cannot be done and where failure would result in either serious loss or a substantial missed opportunity which is unlikely to occur again.*

Your first step, therefore, is to check that your project really is a crisis project.

1. Is the deadline less than a week away? This may seem an arbitrary rule, but I impose it with good reason. The 'quick and dirty' approach to project management outlined in this chapter has one crucial limitation – it is not sustainable. That is, it will work for a brief period, but will fall apart if you attempt to apply it for anything longer than a week.

2. Is the project one which commonsense suggests cannot be achieved? If not, there is no need to resort to crisis methods.

3. Are the consequences of failure sufficiently serious to justify defining the project as a crisis? The approach described in this

chapter is hard work, demanding of resources and disruptive to other activity. This is all very well when you have a genuine emergency, and the results will more than justify the costs, but is clearly not workable on a regular basis. A good way to think about this is to ask yourself what is likely to happen if you just ignore the situation. There will be a few occasions when the consequences really would be catastrophic, but in many cases the truth is that it would not have that great an impact. This is not to say that you should not do it, merely that it may not justify declaring a full-scale crisis.

The 'constant crisis' culture

In action, be primitive; in foresight, a strategist.

René Char

In some organizations crisis is a part of the culture. Even the simplest task is turned into a crisis by virtue of poor planning, inefficient working practices or inadequate resources. Events which could have been predicted and planned for months ago are suddenly happening next week. Decisions which should have been researched and considered last year are suddenly forced on someone today. A project which could be completed in a relaxed fashion by using the appropriate human and technical resources becomes a crisis because someone is demanding it be done by one inexperienced person with little or no organizational support. And so on and so on and so on.

If you work in such an organization, my advice would be change the culture within your own department, or get out. Do not be tempted to apply the crisis-management tools described here. You are already in a 'no-win' situation, and taking a crisis-management approach to something that is not actually a crisis, and which will be followed by another imitation crisis next week, will only make the situation worse.

STOP!

In times of crisis, the temptation to jump straight into action is almost irresistible. It feels as if there is no time to define objectives, plan the project or brief people properly.

In reality, nothing could be further from the truth: when you have plenty of time available, you can afford to allow things to go wrong;

you can always start again. When faced with a crisis there is no time to start again – you have to get it right first time. Careful planning is thus absolutely key to successful crisis management.

Define your objectives

As with any project, you need to start by defining your objective. Run it through the tests in Chapter 1: when you cannot afford to waste a single moment, you want to be certain that every ounce of effort counts. Examine your objective particularly to see whether you really need to achieve as much as that. Can the objective be simplified, made easier to achieve, and still perform its job?

Identify the critical success factors

Once you have your objective, identify the critical success factors – the key goals that must be achieved in order to complete the project successfully. Again, the aim here is to separate the essential from the disposable. For example, if you need to prepare a tender document by 10 a.m. tomorrow morning, does it need to contain the detailed technical specifications? Could you state that it will meet certain listed standards, and that detailed specifications will be made available on request? This would dramatically reduce the work required to be completed by the deadline.

Choose your team

Always try to work with people you know and have worked with before. Forming good working relationships takes time, and time is the one ingredient you do not have during a crisis.

Ideally, of course, you will assign your best people to the project. But even if you do not have this luxury, it is easier to work with a known quantity than an unknown one. At least you know their strengths and weaknesses, and can factor these into the project. The unexpected is the greatest danger when time is tight.

Consider calling in outside consultants. They can often prove extremely cost-effective during short-term, high-velocity projects. But again, wherever possible choose consultants you know and have worked with before.

If the project involves a number of people, hand pick the team leaders and give them the authority to hand pick their own teams.

Plan the project

If you are already familiar with the timeline system detailed in Chapter 2, perhaps because you have used it on several projects by the time the crisis arises, use the same system, but keep it extremely simple. You will, of course, be working in days – or even hours – rather than weeks. You do not need to break every milestone down into detailed actions on the timeline – just ensure that the person or team responsible for each milestone knows exactly what it is they need to achieve.

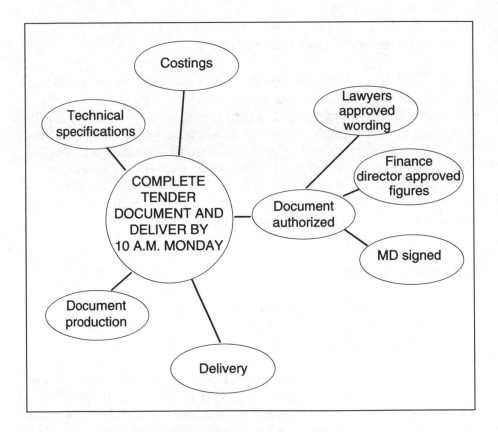

Figure 10.1 A 'mind-map' of critical success factors

If you are not yet familiar with this timelining system, I suggest you try a process known as 'mind-mapping'. Developed by Tony Buzan, mind-mapping enables you to cope with a multitude of complex information while still retaining a clear overview of the project as a whole. You can use it on your own, but where the team comprises up to five or six people, it is often more effective to create the mind-map with your project team.

Take a large sheet of paper – A2 is ideal. Write the objective in capital letters in the middle of the sheet, and draw a circle around it. Next, write down your critical success factors around this circle, using a different colour pen for each one, as shown in Figure 10.1.

Draw circles around these critical success factors. Now take each in turn, and write the key actions required to achieve each critical success factor. Use the same colour pen for this whole 'branch' of the project. Again, circle each one and draw lines linking them to the critical success factor.

Like the timelining system used in Chapter 2, you are free to jump back and forth between the different areas of the project if you suddenly think of something relating to a different branch.

Once you have completed the mind-map, assign each critical success factor to a different individual or group, and let them plan their own actions.

Use appropriate yardsticks

There is no room for perfectionism in a crisis. No matter how passionate your commitment to excellence, your operating principle in a crisis needs to be 'good enough'. In some areas, 'good enough' may well need to be excellent. If you are preparing a brochure, for example, the standard needs to be consistently high. But in many areas, 'good enough' will be a relatively low standard – much lower than you would normally accept.

Keep asking yourself: What is the minimum acceptable standard for this step in order to satisfy the needs of the project? Work to this standard.

Delegate, delegate, delegate

You are working with a team you know. Trust them. Give them the authority they need to perform their role with minimum reference to you. Set up the minimum monitoring system required (see below), and then leave people to go about their jobs.

147

As project manager, you should be doing almost none of the day-to-day work. When time is tight, it is crucial that one person – you – maintains an overview of the project, and is available to trouble-shoot as required. You cannot do either if you are busy with your own tasks. Delegate everything that can be delegated, and then delegate the rest.

Having delegated, consider yourself the servant of the team, not the master. Always look at how you can support your team in doing the job. Do they need greater authority, additional resources, a pat on the back, some words of advice . . . ? Your job is to give them whatever they need to succeed, and to maintain an overview of the project – not to become embroiled in its detail.

Create a simple monitoring system

You need a method of monitoring project progress, but you want to keep paperwork to an absolute minimum. The simplest system is to ask your team to give you a daily summary of progress: what has been achieved today, and what remains to be done. This can be written or oral, but needs to be brief and to the point – no more than a few sentences.

Make it clear that you only want to know *what* is going on, not *why*. Unless someone needs your help in solving a problem, you do not have time to listen to long explanations about why something was delayed, you only want to know whether the problem has been identified and solved.

If you have a large team, keep a simple 'school register' tick-list of your team members. Place a tick against each person when you have received their daily status report. If you have not heard from someone for a day, contact him or her: people tend to hide when things go wrong. Let your team know that your only concern is getting the project completed. You are not going to blame anyone if something goes wrong, you just need to know if the team members run into anything they have not been able to solve so that you can assign additional resources to the problem.

Create simple project maps

You do not have time to create the kind of pretty or creative project maps you would use in a standard project, but even if it is just a big thermometer-style 'percentage complete' gauge on a whiteboard, coloured in with a felt marker, use something to show your team what progress is being made.

Involve everyone

Let all and sundry know what you are doing. Help can always come from the most unexpected quarters, doubly so in a crisis.

Do not be afraid to demand a lot from people. Ask them for what you really want, not what you think would be reasonable to ask of them. Several project managers have told me of times when they asked for something they did not really expect to be delivered, but their team took it in their stride. People are often willing to work long hours on a crisis project as long as they know that their work is appreciated.

Call in all your favours! If you have used the approaches suggested in Chapter 5, you will have developed good working relationships with people. Now is the time to benefit from those relationships. Ask suppliers to pull out all the stops for you. Ask your family to be tolerant while you work long hours. Find out if colleagues in other departments can offer any assistance. Even business contacts in other organizations may be willing to help.

Well-being

Most healthy people can cope with up to a week of hard work without ill effect. You can thus safely suspend your normal rules about working hours, sleep, exercise, diet and so on. But even so, you still need limits: while it is possible, very occasionally, to work 20 hours non-stop, you cannot do this for five days in a row and still produce effective work, for example.

Keep an eye on the well-being of your team, also. If someone has ceased to work effectively, or is consistently short-tempered, this is usually a warning sign that they are neglecting their well-being. Even in a crisis, both they and the project will be better off if they go home and sleep rather than working themselves into the ground.

In general

Always look for the simplest possible solution. If a step is proving more complicated or time-consuming than expected, look for a simpler way to achieve the same end. If a step is completely stuck, ask yourself if you really need to achieve it at all – whether there is some alternative that will do the job. The key to success is to keep the project moving at all times. Deal with obstacles right away. Make decisions immediately. Beg, steal or borrow whatever resources are needed – including people.

After the crisis

The temptation immediately after a crisis has been averted is to breathe a huge sigh of relief and immediately set out to catch up on your regular work. Resist this temptation for a moment! There are three remaining steps which are every bit as much a part of crisis-management as the actions performed before the deadline.

First, thank all those people who made it possible. Remember to include those not on the team itself – colleagues in other departments, suppliers, outside consultants and so on.

Second, schedule time in your diary to spend a few minutes speaking individually with each member of the team, letting them know that their personal contribution was appreciated.

Finally, if people have had to work long hours, give everyone involved – including yourself – a day's paid leave. Even if the department is busy anyway, they will work more efficiently for a day's rest and relaxation.

SUMMARY

- The first step is to ensure that you really are facing a crisis. The approach detailed in this chapter is suitable only where the deadline is no more than a week away, where normal working practices would not get the job done and where the consequences of failing to complete the project would either be a serious loss or a substantial missed opportunity.

- Beware of organizations which exist in a 'culture crisis,' where everything becomes a crisis through poor planning, inefficient working methods or inadequate resources. Again, this approach is not suitable for frequent pseudo-crises.

- When time is short, defining your objectives and planning the project is more important than ever: there is no time to start again if your initial attempt does not work.

- Identify the critical success factors necessary to achieve the objective, and forget everything else. Check for actions which appear critical, but which could actually wait until after the project deadline.

- Always aim to work with a team you know. There is no time to form a good working relationship from scratch. Consider using outside consultants, but again aim to use ones you know.

- Plan your project using either a simplified version of the *Getting Results* timeline, or the mind-mapping approach described in this chapter. Assign each track or branch of the project to a specific individual or team, and let them plan it in detail.

- Delegate, delegate, delegate. You must remain free to maintain an overview of progress, and to trouble-shoot as required. Give your team the authority they need to do their jobs effectively with minimal reference to you.

- Keep your project monitoring system simple. Ask for oral reports, or written ones limited to a few sentences. Let people know you only want to be told the *what*, not the *why* – unless they need your help in solving a problem.

- Create a simple project map – a thermometer-style 'percentage complete' map can be created on a whiteboard in a matter of minutes.

- Involve everyone. Call in favours. Demand more of people than you consider reasonable – they will often surprise you.

- Relax your well-being rules, but use your commonsense. Keep an eye on the well-being of your team.

- Keep looking for simpler and faster solutions. If something is stuck, find a different way of achieving the same end. Keep the project moving at all costs.

- Beg, steal or borrow resources – including people – as you need them.

- Complete three steps after the crisis is over: thank the team as a whole, schedule time to thank each person individually, and give everyone – including yourself – a day's paid leave.

11

HELP!

or It never rains but it pours

There are very few certainties in project management, but this is one of them: things will go wrong.

This is good news if you are a project manager, since it is what keeps you in employment. If projects always ran according to plan, you would have a few days' work drawing up the initial plan and the organization could then dispense with your services.

Problems are also the ingredients that make the difference between a job that is routine, perhaps dull, and one which offers constant challenge and excitement. Tackled properly, it is the unexpected problems that offer the greatest potential for job satisfaction; it may be satisfying to look back on a project and congratulate yourself on the fact that everything went exactly the way you had planned, but it is far more satisfying to look back on how you successfully recovered from potential disaster.

I was once responsible for arranging to obtain and deliver 15 000 lightbulbs to a Romanian town which was going to be in darkness for its first Christmas as a democracy. The project, the idea of a newspaper journalist and television crew, was sprung on us just 48 hours before the truck had to leave. Thirty-six hours later, we had everything in place: truck, drivers, lightbulbs, ferry passage, chase car, paperwork . . . and the next day we set off on the 2 500-mile round-trip.

The project was immensely satisfying. But some of ·the real highlights of the trip were the moments when disaster threatened, and we had to do some fast thinking to solve an unexpected problem. The moment, literally hours before we were due to leave, when the truck company heard reports of civil unrest in Romania and withdrew its offer of both truck and drivers . . . The point at which, with 20 minutes to go before our ferry left, the promised free tickets had apparently been lost in the system . . . the moment we arrived in Romania in sub-zero temperatures after driving non-stop for two days and two nights to find that our accommodation did not exist . . . the point where we found that we did not have enough carnets (customs documents) to bring the television camera safely back to the UK . . . It was solving these problems that gave us the most satisfaction, rather than the parts that ran according to plan.

This chapter cannot solve your problems for you. It cannot even offer much practical guidance on how to go about solving the problems you will face, since just about any area of a project can go wrong. What it can do, fundamentally, is to present a proven *approach* – an 'attitude of mind' – not only to coping with problems, but actually coming to enjoy doing so.

The job is not to get it right

> It is not the critic who counts; not the man who points out how the strong man stumbled or where the doer of deeds could have done them better. The credit belongs to the man who is actually in the arena, whose face is marred with dust and sweat and blood; who strives valiantly; who errs and comes short again and again; who knows the great enthusiasms, the great devotion; who spends himself in a worthy cause; who, at the best, knows the triumph of high achievement and, at the worst, at least fails while daring greatly.
>
> Theodore Roosevelt

The job of a project manager is not to ensure that events match the project plan in every last detail. This has never happened to even the very best of project managers, and never will. The job is to ensure that you succeed in achieving the project objective by any means at your disposal. If it happens that a section of the project plan does its job perfectly, that is great. But if not, this is not cause for depression or panic: it is simply a signal that you need to take immediate action to produce the same result by other means.

Succeeding with a project really does have as much to do with an attitude of mind as it does with specific skills and abilities. Sir John Harvey-Jones put it very succinctly once: 'There are too few bombastic people who believe they can do anything'. There is almost nothing that cannot be achieved through determination and confidence.

Confidence, like panic, is contagious. As project manager, your first and most important job when things go wrong is to maintain the faith in the success of the project of those around you. They will look to you for a lead, not only in terms of what to do but also in terms of how to respond. If you panic, so will they; if you approach the problem calmly and decisively, so will those around you.

Of course, being calm and decisive is not the easiest of states of mind to achieve when you genuinely do not have a clue what to do! The first thing is to give yourself some breathing space. There are usually some immediate steps you can take, even if you are not sure how to tackle the whole problem. Do you have all the information you need, for example? Do you know exactly what has gone wrong, and what consequences this will have? If not, delegate the task of obtaining this information to someone on your team. Is an immediate stop-gap measure required? Again, delegate this task.

While your team takes care of the immediate steps, give yourself some time to think. But do not do any unnecessary thinking. This might seem odd advice to give, but most of us have an 'automatic' response when something goes wrong: we want to know how it happened, we want to know whose fault it was and we want to know what we could have done to prevent it happening. Assigning blame is rarely useful; working out how something happened and how it can be prevented on future projects is useful, but you can leave this until after the project is complete. The only thing you need to know now is what action you will take to solve the immediate problem.

When considering the action you need to take, be willing to ignore the original plan. It may be necessary to tackle the problem in a completely different way, either because the planned method has demonstrated itself to be unsuitable, or simply because you no longer have the time or resources necessary to take the planned approach. Much of the advice given in Chapter 10 will be useful here also: look for the 'critical success factors', the factors that make a noticeable difference, apply the principle of 'good enough for the job' and always look for a simpler way of achieving the same results.

If you cannot quickly arrive at a solution yourself, ask for advice. Can any of your 'extended team' (as defined in Chapter 5) be of help? Does your team have anything to suggest? You will have to apply your own judgement here on who and how to ask: you want to benefit from the expertise and creativity available to you, but you do not want to panic people by appearing to have no idea what to do. You will normally have a good idea who will be helpful and who would merely panic.

If a particular step in the project is posing real problems, and you cannot find a way to deal with it, ask yourself whether the step could be either postponed or even omitted. For example, if you had planned to include name badges in the pre-event packs mailed to participants, could you instead have the badges waiting for them on arrival? Or if you had planned to include a booking form for reduced-price accommodation at the hotel, could you instead just include the hotel phone number and ask the hotel to handle the bookings directly?

Act quickly, maintain momentum

It is important to act quickly. If you have to choose between a number of possible solutions to the problem, give yourself enough time to think clearly, but do not spend *too* much time analysing the relative merits of each. It is better to make an imperfect decision promptly than to make a perfect decision too late to implement it.

Once you have decided how you will tackle the problem, act immediately. Delegate the solution to one member of your team, provide him or her with the resources he or she needs and re-assign his or her other work. Once you have done so, return your attention to the project as a whole. If you get diverted into dealing with one particular aspect yourself, you will not be able to maintain an effective overview of the project and will almost certainly run into further problems.

Make sure that the rest of the project maintains momentum. It is easy to pay so much attention, and divert so many resources, to dealing with a problem that the rest of the project begins to suffer.

Look ahead

I said earlier that you should postpone an analysis of how things went wrong until after the project is complete. There is one exception to this, and that is if there is any likelihood of the same, or similar, failure happening again later in the project.

For example, if a printer was late delivering the brochures for a conference, and you are relying on that same printer to deliver the conference programmes on time, you will want to ensure that the same problem does not recur.

Look through the rest of your timeline. Is there any point where you might be faced with a similar problem? If so, take steps now to avert it.

Also, ask yourself whether your new solution to the problem in hand might itself have implications for the rest of the project. For example, if you decided to omit a computer graphics presentation in order to keep the project on track, do you need to alter the conference programme accordingly?

Crises

If you have an exceptionally serious problem, consider putting the project on a crisis footing as a temporary measure, applying the crisis management approach described in Chapter 10. Remember that this can be done for a maximum of one week – it is a 'last resort' approach – but it can be used to solve some immediate problems and to get the project back on track.

Don't panic!

Finally, remember that the project manager has the most depressing view of the project! You can see every flaw, you know every problem, you know exactly where the reality differed from the theory. Many of the events you consider disastrous – because they fail to match your expectations – will not even be noticed by the people who matter: the customers.

Conference delegates, for example, do not know that they should have seen a wonderfully impressive display of computer graphics instead of the more pedestrian slides they actually saw. As far as they are concerned, the way it went is the way it was supposed to go.

Even on the rare occasions when a problem is obvious to all – a failed microphone, for example – the customers will rarely consider it as serious a failure as it appears to you. To you, it is an unmitigated disaster; to the delegates it was either a minor irritation (you did have a replacement mike standing by, did you not?) or – at worst – something to joke about over lunch. By all means do everything you can to have the project run as flawlessly as possible, but recognize that perfection only exists in the story books, and when a problem has happened and been handled, forget about it until after the project.

Maintain your sense of humour. Even the most apparently irredeemable situations have solutions if you do not allow yourself to be panicked into inactivity. An after-dinner speaker told the story of a time when he suddenly realized that not a single person was listening to a word he was saying. The entire audience was clearly bored out if its collective mind. And he had another 20 minutes left to go. He stopped talking. The audience began to wake up and wonder what was happening. He then stepped down from the podium, and walked to the back of the room. By this time, every eye was on him. He went out of the room, and nothing happened for 30 seconds. The room was silent. The delegates then heard the sound of a toilet flushing, the speaker returned to the room, walked back up to the podium and carried on from where he had left off. From that moment on, he had the rapt attention of every person in the room.

Look on even the most nightmarish problem as a challenge. Take a deep breath, allow yourself to see the funny side and then tell yourself that it is for moments like this that you receive your pay. And remember that a month from now the situation will make a terrific after-dinner story.

SUMMARY

- Things will go wrong. If they did not, there would be no need for project managers. Something going wrong is not a sign that you are not able to do the job, it is just a signal that corrective action is required.

- There is limited satisfaction in a project that runs completely to plan. It is pleasing in a quiet way, but the real satisfaction – and post-project entertainment value – arises from the times when events definitely did not go according to plan and you applied all your ingenuity to finding an effective solution.

- The job of a project manager is not to get it right, but to achieve the project objective by any means available to you. It is ultimately irrelevant whether or not you did so by following your original plan.

- Confidence, like panic, is contagious. The project manager's first job in a crisis is to maintain everyone's faith in the success of the project. Approach problems calmly and decisively (even if you feel anything but), and those around you will do the same.

- Do not waste time wondering why it happened or whose fault it was. You can learn your lessons once the project is complete; right now the only thing that matters is finding a solution. The only exception to this is to ask yourself whether a similar problem could occur later in the project; if so, identify the cause and take steps to avert future problems.

- When you are not sure what to do, look for obvious immediate steps. Do you need more information on the problem? Is there an obvious stop-gap measure? Delegate these immediate steps to your team while you create some breathing space for yourself.

- Be willing to ask for advice.

- If something is posing a tricky problem, ask yourself whether that action could be postponed or even omitted, as in the badge and hotel examples in this chapter.

- It is better to make an imperfect decision promptly than a perfect one too late to implement it.

- Once you have made your decision, delegate the required action while you maintain your attention on the project as a whole and ensure that the rest of the project maintains momentum.

- In exceptional cases, consider putting the project on a crisis footing as a temporary measure, using the crisis management approach presented in Chapter 10. But do not do so unless, and for any longer than, absolutely necessary.

- Remember that the project manager has the most depressing view of the project. It looks a hundred times better to everyone else.

12

AFTER THE PROJECT

or Never again!

Experience is not what happens to you. It is what you do with what
happens to you.

Aldous Huxley

The project is complete. What worked, worked; what didn't, didn't.
You may feel delighted at the accomplishment; relieved that it is all
over; annoyed at what went wrong; you may even feel a kind of
'post-project depression' – a sense of anti-climax that the thing you
have worked on for so long is over so quickly. Or any mixture of
these thoughts.

Do not read too much into any of these feelings: they are all part and
parcel of the business of completing a project. Particularly so if you
feel unhappy about the way anything went; as I said in Chapter 11,
the project manager is the least qualified person to make any kind of
judgement about how it went. Your project team, too, is poorly
placed to evaluate the overall success of the project. If you want to
know whether or not, on balance, the project succeeded or failed,
ask the customer. The participants in the conference, the
beneficiaries of the marketing campaign, the people who use the
new computer system.

Do not ask for detailed feedback at this stage, just for a general
opinion on whether or not it worked. And believe the answers you
are given! Remember, what is important is not whether the reality
matched the plan, but whether the 'customer' liked the result.

Celebrate and relax

The biggest favour you can do yourself in preparing yourself for your next project is to invest a little more time in this one: handling the action steps that take place *after* the objective has been achieved. These will not take long, but will repay you many times over when you come to tackle future – perhaps much bigger – projects.

The first such action is to do nothing for a day or two. Take some time off, and have your project team do the same. Relax and enjoy the sense of accomplishment – you have all earned it!

The amount of time you should take off will depend on the length and pace of the project. If you have been working hard for six months, you may want to take a week or two off; if you have been working at a reasonable level for a couple of weeks, a morning may be enough, but do take some time.

Thank everyone

Your project would not have been possible without the work of your immediate team, and the support of your 'extended' team: colleagues, senior management, customers, family and friends. Use your project manual to make a list of all the people who played a part in the success of the project (the diagram you did of your 'lines of communication' in Chapter 5 will also be helpful here), and write down alongside each a key phrase for the contribution that that person made to the project. It may be a specific time when he or she went to a lot of trouble, it may be a specific result he or she pulled off, or it may be a quality he or she exhibited throughout the project – perhaps remaining calm in time of crisis, always breaking the tension with a joke or being willing to take on any job if it would move the project forward.

Use this list to give everyone a personal 'thank you' for their help. You might do this by dropping round to see them, giving them a call or sending them a card. Sending a card with just a line or two letting people know how much you appreciated their support may seem like a very small thing to do, but it is usually appreciated much more than you might expect – especially by the people we normally forget to thank, like outside suppliers.

Thanking people is not only a courtesy, it will pay dividends next time you need to ask for help. You will usually find these people very ready to assist next time simply because they know that their contribution is appreciated.

The earlier you thank people, the more impact it will have. This should thus be the first step you take after taking time off. A thank you while the project is still fresh and alive in people's minds really means something; a thank you a month or so later, when it is just a dim memory and they are busy working on another project, has a very limited impact.

Tie up loose ends

Are there any loose ends in the project? For example, did you put alternative suppliers on standby in case your main supplier let you down? If so, contact these suppliers to let them know that the project is complete and that you did not need their help, and thank them for being ready in reserve.

Run through your timeline, checking for loose ends, and complete them as required.

Close the budget

A budget will be useful in future only if it is closed at the end of the project, and you can refer to the total costs. Very often, project managers wait for every last invoice to arrive before closing the project. Since there will always be one or two bills that do not arrive for months, this can easily mean that the budget is never completed at all. By the time the final bills arrive, you are too busy with your next project.

Set yourself a cut-off date no later than a month after the project objective is achieved, and close the project at this point. If there are any outstanding bills, phone suppliers and ask for the figures. If any figures are not available, use your best estimate: a total which is out by one or two per cent is much more useful than a budget which has no total at all.

Write your reports

If you have any reports to write, do them now, while the project is still fresh in your mind. This not only means that you are more likely to remember important details, but writing a report immediately after the event can be extremely satisfying, as you put down in black-and-white exactly what was achieved. Left to later, it will simply become a chore distracting you from your current project.

Complete the project manual

Similar logic applies to the project manual. Completing it now means that it will be an accurate record of what happened. Details which are vivid in your mind now will fade within a few weeks. Even points you are sure you could never forget will lose their urgency after a month or two.

Hold a 'post mortem'

A project 'post mortem' (a rather gruesome title!) is a meeting in which the project team takes an objective look at what did and did not work. Its purpose is not to assign blame, or to worry about what happened – it is all history now – but instead, to pick out the lessons that can be learned for next time.

To be effective, a post mortem should take place within a week or two of the project end, but not *too* soon. There is an interim period in which everyone is too closely bound up in the project, and not yet able to look objectively at it. That is why I suggest that this meeting takes place after the above actions have taken place.

A post mortem meeting needs to walk a fine line between glossing over important points on the one side, and dwelling on past mistakes on the other. It should allow everyone an opportunity to contribute, but must not degenerate into useless discussion about what did or did not happen. The key to the success of the meeting is that it must be geared to looking at the future more than the past: comments should be constructive suggestions for avoiding difficulties in future, not a laboured discourse on what happened during this project.

When I edited a magazine, we held a monthly post mortem meeting for each issue. The magazine was 64 pages long, and the meetings rarely lasted longer than an hour – an average of less than a minute per page. We achieved this by asking everyone to check through the magazine prior to the meeting, and highlight both errors and any more general suggestions they wanted to raise. During the meeting itself, we would transfer all the identified errors on to a single copy of the magazine, so that we could take steps to prevent similar errors occurring in the next issue, and reach rapid decisions on any suggestions people had to make. The pace of the meeting meant that there was no time for any non-constructive comments, and everybody knew this.

Assign one person the role of secretary to the meeting. This person is responsible for taking notes on all the decisions reached, for summarizing these in written form and distributing them to all those involved.

Once you have this document, do not just file it and forget it, but keep it in your project manual and refer to it before you plan your next project. It is amazing how often we repeat the same mistakes unless we take positive steps to ensure that old lessons are incorporated into future projects.

Evaluate the project

The final step in completing the project is for the organization to ask itself the $64 000 question: was it all worth it?

By this, I do not mean your personal feelings about the project, but an objective look at the cost-benefit analysis on which the project was based. Given the *actual* costs of the project, as opposed to those estimated at the outset, and the *actual* value of the benefits delivered, as opposed to those anticipated in the initial plan, how did the project fair?

You may not be able to answer this question immediately. If the project was a marketing campaign, for example, it may be 12 months before you can compare the level of sales achieved with those achieved in the same quarter last year. If so, make a note now to carry out this evaluation at the appropriate time.

It is essential that you understand that this is a different question to the one you asked earlier: was the project successful? In asking that question, you were evaluating your performance as a project manager. Did you pull off the project to a satisfactory standard? In asking 'was it worth it?', you are asking a question that has little or nothing to do with your own performance. You are asking whether the organization made the right decision in going ahead with the project in the first place.

Like the post mortem, the purpose of asking this question is for future reference. Whether the answer is yes or no, you began the project with the information available to you then, not the information you have available with the benefit of hindsight. If the answer is 'no', it does not mean you should not have undertaken the project, merely that you will be better placed to evaluate similar projects in the future.

And for your own part, the answer to this question is largely irrelevant. Your job was to complete the project successfully. If you did that, you have the right to call yourself a successful project manager whether or not the organization would undertake a similar project in future.

SUMMARY

- You may experience a wide range of emotions at the end of a project, from elation to depression. Do not read too much into these feelings – they are part and parcel of completing a project.

- Remember that you are the least-qualified person to evaluate the success of the project. Pay attention to the views of the people who count – the 'customers' (internal or external).

- The first thing you need to do after the project is nothing! Take some time to relax and enjoy the sense of accomplishment. And make sure your project team does the same.

- Thank everyone. Drop in to see them, give them a call, send them a thank-you card. This is not only a courtesy, but will pay dividends in future projects – people are always much more willing to help if they know their contribution is appreciated. Thank people earlier rather than later, when the impact is greatest.

- Tie up any loose ends. For example, did you ask alternative suppliers to place themselves on standby in case they were needed?

- Close the budget. Set yourself a cut-off date by which you will produce the final budget, no later than a month from now. If you do not have all the bills in by then, ask suppliers for the figures. Estimate the cost of any unknowns: a total containing a few estimated figures is far more useful than a budget which is never completed because a few bills remain outstanding.

- Write up all your reports as soon as possible, and complete your project manual. Done now, this will add to your sense of satisfaction; left until later, it will become a chore.

- Hold a 'post mortem' meeting: an objective look at what did and did not work. Remember that the aim of this meeting is to identify lessons for next time, not to dwell on the past.

- Evaluate the project by looking afresh at the cost-benefit analysis now that the true costs and benefits are known. Remember that this evaluation does not tell you how well you did your job, just whether or not the organization would undertake a similar project in future.

INDEX